ENGINES
GOOD and BAD

ENGINES
GOOD and BAD

A. W. Summers

Oxford Publishing Company

Typesetting by:
Aquarius Typesetting Services, New Milton, Hants.

Printed in Great Britain by:
Hollen Street Press Ltd., Slough, Berks.

Published by:
Oxford Publishing Co.
Link House
West Street
POOLE, Dorset

CHAPTER ONE

I left school in July 1921, at the age of thirteen years and eleven months and, like many other young people I felt that at last I was someone. I do not now remember if my parents took a daily newspaper, but if they did, and if I had read the news daily, I think now that I would have preferred to have been much younger.

The uppermost thought in my mind, after suffering the school leavers' ceremony with a kindly chat from the headmaster, was that now I could go out into industry and make something of myself. My memory was good, I was good on the drawing board and generally I had no fears concerning the possibility of my progressing. However, my elder brother was working only three days a week, and this should have warned me of what was to come. However, at fourteen, I did not realise that there were any problems; I just had my own ideas.

The industrial areas of London around where I lived in Harlesden — Willesden, Acton, Park Royal and Shepherd's Bush — employed thousands of people, and the road in which I lived, lined with bay-windowed houses each containing two flats, was where some of them resided. In this road, 80 per cent of the people were unemployed; how they all envied the two policemen, one postman and three engine drivers who lived amongst us.

After job hunting for three months, I began to realise that there was a problem, although I did get my first job, at 14s. 7½d. a week, feeding a machine in a factory. That did not last very long as the factory was soon closed down, and I was reduced to taking an errand boy's job in High Road, Brondesbury. This was at a chemist's shop, for which I was paid 15s. a week. I began to get quite interested in the chemist's work and decided that I wanted to be a chemist, until I realised that I would need money to train for this profession. The money was not forthcoming, and very soon that job also came to an end. Like thousands of others, I was again unemployed.

Then, in May 1923, the Government appealed to the four main line railway companies to take on more engine cleaners, in an attempt to reduce the juvenile unemployed. My experience of railways up until then had been limited. I can still remember, at the age of nine or ten, sitting in the field opposite the main gate to Old Oak Common Locomotive Shed and watching the workmen come out at night, just as the roar of the 5.30p.m. 'going home' hooter died away. At other times we would climb on to the level crossing gates, close to fields at Acton where we used to play, and watch the LSWR goods trains passing. Those LSWR 4-4-0s had huge churning driving wheels and were an awe inspiring sight. I wonder, in retrospect, if any of them ended their days on the Didcot to Winchester passenger trains with that little boy, now grown to manhood, at the regulator?

In the flat above us lived Wilfred Flaxman, a GWR engine driver. His wife and my mother were very friendly, and my mother told me one day that Mr Flaxman, had suggested recommending me for a job on the railway. I cannot recall that, at any time previously, I had felt that I wanted to become an engine driver. This seemed to me to be one of those things that was so remote that it just could not happen, so I had never really considered it. Soon afterwards, however, I found myself in the waiting-room of the main office block at Old Oak Common. With me was Driver Flaxman, in full working kit, to show on whose recommendation I had reached this stage. With us were 25 other boys, all about the same age, with their sponsors.

Gradually the room began to get less crowded and, as names were called alphabetically, I was one of the last. By the time it was my turn I was feeling a bit nervous; so much depended upon my getting steady work that I began to fidget, but after a timely word from Mr Flaxman I was fully at ease again. Eventually I was called and was asked many questions, and all my answers were true and given smartly; but there was one question — 'have you any relations working for the Great Western Railway?' — to which I could not give an answer in the affirmative. This, I noticed, brought a frown to the questioner's face. I was told to wait outside, and my friend Driver Flaxman was called in. He was only inside for a couple of minutes and then we were on our way home. I felt sure that the quickness of Mr Flaxman's exit was an indication that I had failed my interview. But he said, 'Alf, you have been selected to take your test and medical at Swindon. You will be sent for!'

Time passed and nothing happened or, at least, nothing seemed to happen. In the meantime my father died, which made it all the more important that I should get employment on a steady and continuous basis. Then, after what seemed like ages, one morning — I remember it as though it were yesterday — my mother brought into my bedroom a letter; on the back of the envelope was the coat of arms of the Great Western Railway. Inside was a simple little note which said, 'You will report to Park House, Swindon on 7th July for a general knowledge and medical examination. Please bring 2/6 entry fee for the GWR Medical and Superannuation Scheme which you will be required to join on passing your medical.' There followed instructions on which train to travel by and directions to Park House, where the examination would be held, from Swindon Station. Also enclosed was a free return ticket for the journey.

I was no stranger to rail travel, having gone by the Broad Street line to High Road, Brondesbury, during my previous employment at the chemist's shop. However, this was something different. I was very impressed how, after passing Slough, the surrounding country took on a rural appearance, but as can be easily imagined, this was only a passing fantasy as my thoughts were centred on the coming examination at Swindon. Yet again I had no reason to be pessimistic, as I was confident that my educational standards were quite good, and I could think of no physical defects to prevent my passing the medical.

On arrival at Swindon, I found the directions given in the letter quite adequate, and soon found myself in the waiting-room at Park House, along with about thirty other chaps all about my age. The different dialects were most amusing; there were some from Devon and Cornwall and also a few from Wales although, in the main, the London accent predominated.

The general knowledge, writing, composition and eyesight examinations were taken first by the various inspectors. Whilst those of us whose names were near to the end of the alphabet waited, we knew, that when anyone returned from the examinations, collected his hat and coat and departed, in most cases without a word, that they had failed for one reason or another. Hence I have always thought to remember that room as the 'valley of tears'. Then it was my turn.

It will, I think, be sufficient to say here that immediately after taking these tests I was directed to the medical waiting-room where, once more, the whole procedure seemed to repeat itself. I have, over a number of years, had many medical examinations, but this really was something to be remembered forever; in fact, I would say that it was unforgettable. The thoroughness of it all suddenly came home to me when the doctor told me that he could not pass me beause I had a decayed tooth, but that if I chose to go to the dentist during the dinner break and have it removed, he would be satisfied. I was astonished at this statement but, fortunately, I did not question it. I feel sure that had I done so I would have been on my way home immediately afterwards. However, I must mention that I had always taken great care of my teeth, and had never seen a mark of decay on any of them. Therefore, instead of partaking of dinner, I went to a local dentist first. I was not really surprised when he asked which tooth it was that I wanted extracted. As I remembered the doctor at

Park House touching what he said was the bad tooth, I told the dentist that it was that one. His reaction was that he could not take out a good tooth although, after some persuasion, he agreed to do so, but most reluctantly. Shortly after my return to Park House I was called for by the doctor, who appeared quite satisfied now that I had a gaping hole in my mouth where a double tooth had once been! The reader will probably want to know the purpose behind this business of the tooth. I can only think that this was one way of eliminating candidates whose parents had no connection with the GWR, for that company gave first and almost its only consideration to such people. For the reason behind that policy in itself, I can only leave the reader to judge for himself.

Leaving the doctor I returned to the briefing rooms and, along with five others from London, received instructions about the train for returning home. We were not officially told that we had passed as engine cleaners, but our instructor gave us some very broad hints which made this pretty clear. Having just completed everything required of us, we had every reason to believe him. I returned to Paddington and to my mother's home in Harlesden and, a few days later, received a letter from the GWR instructing me to report to Old Oak Common locomotive shed at 8a.m., to begin my employment as an engine cleaner. Such was my exhilaration at having obtained employment that, on the great day, I paid careful attention to my appearance, being pronounced 'presentable' by my mother. As the last note of the 8a.m. hooter died away, I took my seat once more in the waiting-room at Old Oak Common locomotive shed, along with five others. We did not have long to wait before we were shepherded into the shed itself, and handed over to the engine cleaner's chargehand 'Bert' Smith.

He took us to the engine cleaner's cabin, where he called for the cleaners to come out. To my amazement, about forty men aged from sixteen to about thirty drifted out. It was explained to us that they were split into gangs of four, with a 'captain' to each gang, the 'captain' receiving from the chargehand the number of the engine which his gang had to clean. They then went off to the cleaner's store, where they collected sufficient cotton waste and cleaning oil for the job in hand. I learned later that the copper and brasswork, with which GWR engines were adorned, came up better when cleaned with soot and newspaper.

I was told to work in the gang captained by Frank Burridge who, I think, was about 22. His first reaction was to ask me why I had come dressed up, and naturally I responded by saying that I wished to appear smart and tidy. He agreed with this sentiment, but he said that it would not do here and asked 'have you no overalls to put on over your clothes?'. Of course I had not, so he lent me some of his until I was able to get some of my own.

I understood that on this shift we worked from 8a.m. until 5.45p.m. with a break for dinner from 12.30p.m. until 1.30p.m., and this we did five days a week plus 4¼ hours on Saturday, to complete a 48 hour week. During the dinner break, eight more cleaners arrived in the cabin to start the midday shift. I soon learned that my turns of duty would be the night and day shift alternatively, with one week every twelve weeks on the midday shift.

All this information I gathered very quickly from the other cleaners in my first day or so. They did their best to create a welcoming atmosphere for new cleaners, and as the days passed I found that they were a very grand bunch to work with — about a quarter of them were ex-servicemen, having been engine cleaners since the end of the war. Having settled in I found that our tastes were very nearly identical, and what at first was just a job, lengthened into a satisfying occupation.

Like all employers in those days, the Great Western Railway put great store by punctuality and of course there were occasions when the wrath of the foreman seemed to loom large, and times when I had to run frantically down Tubbs Road towards Willesden Junction Station. I would perhaps be half-way along the road when the locomotive shed steam hooter would blast out two long ear-splitting wails, warning that the time was 7.50a.m. When I had to be on duty at 8a.m. this would be a distinct signal to hurry.

The possibility of catching a tram might be ruled out by the queue of people boarding it just past the corner of Tubbs Road and Station Road. In those circumstances, should one actually be moving and approaching, I would fling myself on to the boarding platform as it went past. On approaching the stop, the conductor, who might be on the open-top deck, would stamp his foot to inform the driver that the tram was full up and we would sail past the queue, over Willesden Junction Bridge and past the LMS railway cottages and men's home lodge. We then passed the Fisherman's Arms, known to all local railmen, and crossed over the canal bridge to Old Oak Lane, where I would alight before the tram had come to a halt. I paid no fare, as the crush on the top platform made it impossible and, anyway, the tram conductors would often regard railwaymen as 'fellow workers', and not demand a fare.

On these occasions, after leaving the tram and running up to and over Old Oak Bridge to the locomotive shed gates, having shouted 'Morning Harry' to the gateman, the hooter would blast out again

OLD OAK COMMON DEPOT

1. Shed Offices
2. Stores and Running Foreman
3. Repair Shop
4. Smithy, with coppersmith and carpenter shop adjacent
5. Cabins and lavatories
6. Boiler washing plant
7. Water softener
8. Sand furnace
9. Coal stage
10. Traverser, with weighbridge immediately beyond

(Official details taken circa 1940)

The sketch below was drawn by the author, from memory, some 30 years after transferring to Didcot.

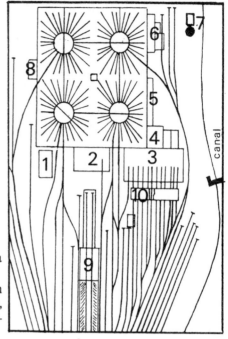

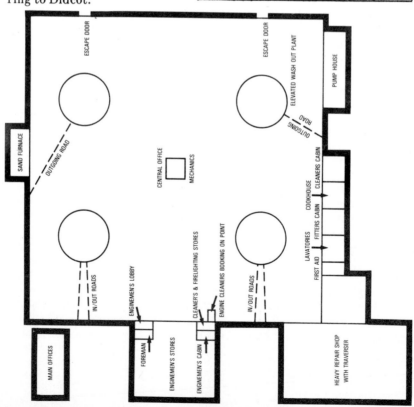

— three long blasts, indicating that it was now 8a.m. You have doubtless heard of people trying to cross Westminster Bridge whilst Big Ben strikes twelve, but perhaps you have never seen workmen running from Old Oak Common Shed gates to the time office whilst the hooter was booming out its 8a.m. wail. Well, I have done that several times, although I was not the only one, down the twisting ash path and into the shed, across the engine turntable (even when the turntable man was operating the electric motor and the table began to turn), jump off the turntable, perhaps just missing an engine pit, and across to the time office just as the last wail died away. I had made it, and another day as an engine cleaner had begun!

Old Oak Depot was a massive place, being the nerve centre of train movements in the London Division and beyond while also housing the offices of the London Division Locomotive Superintendent. Up until 1916, this had been John Armstrong, son of the Locomotive Superintendent who had followed Gooch at Swindon. At the time, of course, the name meant very little to me, but it appears that for years after his retirement, John Armstrong continued to look up his successors at Old Oak Common, so that it is not impossible that in those early years I brushed shoulders with a member of a famous GWR family.

The shed itself was very large, 444ft. by 360ft., with four 65ft. turntables within its walls. Each of these turntables had 28 radiating roads and 112 engine pits in all, with 56 being for tender engines and 56 for tanks. Old Oak Common was the biggest shed on the GWR and was sometimes (surely an exaggeration), called the 'biggest in the world'. Designed by Churchward, as the first of his turntable sheds, it was started in 1902 and took four years to build, replacing the much older depot at Westbourne Park. It became the model for the seven subsequent turntable sheds built on the GWR, although none of them was as big as the first. I am told that they all had points and fixtures to allow other 'standard' sections to be added should it prove necessary. Each approach road was equipped with maintenance pits, and one turntable contained the boiler washer's plant. Light repairs such as piston gland changes, gauge glass and spindle gland removals were carried out in the shed while the heavier work was done in an adjoining building, provided with lifting equipment and plant sufficient for any repair to locomotives large or small.

My first impression of Old Oak Common Shed was that it would be easy to get lost there and, in fact, I can remember that this really did happen. As we were all new boys, practically all engine cleaning was carried out inside the shed, and as all the four turntables looked much the same we had to think hard about where the engine, to which we had been allocated for cleaning, was situated. For the first couple of days, we had to find our way round the shed because it really was a huge building, and each turntable had incoming and outgoing roads which could accommodate every type of locomotive, from a pannier tank to a 'Star', their smokeboxes pointing towards the centre of the turntable. With their numbers on the front buffer beam, it was best to go to the centre of a table and look around at the engines that were visible from that position. It was certainly impossible to walk up and down between the engines because sometimes their cylinder covers, on the big locomotives at least, were very close together.

Amongst the engines stood around these turntables was the towering majesty of the locomotive which I still consider the most magnificent locomotive to have ever been built, Churchward's Pacific *The Great Bear*. This engine figures in a personal experience of mine, from my early days on the railway, when I was cleaning the left-hand side leading bogie of the tender, and noticed that the spring hanger was broken. The driver and fireman were preparing the engine to work the 5.05 service to Bristol, and it was apparent that Driver Wasley had not reached this point yet in his check. It was, of course, normal practice, when a cleaner found a defect, to report it to the driver if he happened to be on the locomotive at the time. Unfortunately, Wasley was always finding fault with the cleaners' work; he would put his hand under the footplate by the driving wheels, and if he found any dirt he would complain to the foreman.

Therefore, upon seeing Bert Smith standing by, I told him of the defect and he immediately sent me to the office to make the appropriate entry in the locomotive fitters' repair book, where all engine repairs were noted for the mechanic's attention. This I did and, on returning to *The Great Bear*, I continued my cleaning. Driver Wasley duly arrived with his oil feeder, and very soon noticed the defective spring hanger. He at once made his way to the office but was soon back, noisily enquiring who Engine Cleaner A. Summers was. After I had enlightened him, he demanded to know why I had not told him of the defect. I should have like to have informed him on that subject, but he knew the reason without asking. To cap it all, and to Wasley's chagrin, I received a handsome gratuity of 5s. for my vigilance (twice the normal amount because it was *The Great Bear*) and my name in the staff commended section of the *GWR Magazine*. Later, *The Great Bear* was sent to Swindon, and broken up in January 1924.

During my early cleaning days, a familiar sight at Old Oak

Common Shed were the three French 'De Glehn' Compound Atlantics, bought by the GWR for comparison with its own express passenger engines. They carried the names *La France*, *Alliance* and *President* which, of course, associated them with the signing of the Entente Cordiale in 1904. To us, they were always the 'Frenchmen'. These engines, however altered by the technical staff at Swindon and given Great Western livery, could not compare with the clean lines of our own engines. Outstanding features of these engines were the three cylinders, the entry half-way up the boiler of the injector delivery pipe and clack box, and the outside valve gear.

The 'Star' class locomotives were some of our worst engines to clean. To clean the back of the big ends, located underneath the locomotive, it was necessary to climb up into what was a very restricted area of space, limited because there was a sand-box situated in the middle of the frame, and this had to be spotless before the driver went underneath to commence oiling. Whilst we always paid special attention to this, even for our own benefit, most drivers donned an old suit of overalls before oiling, because of the rigid rule which said that employees coming into contact with the travelling public had to be smart and tidy at all times.

The first 'Castle' class locomotives arrived at Old Oak Common in the late summer of 1924. Talking to some of our drivers and, especially, the firemen whose everyday experience was regular working on these engines, I formed a picture in my mind of a very powerful locomotive, capable of very fast speeds. I am sure that I do not need to recall the exploits of these engines, particularly of Nos. 5000 or 5005, on that famous train the 'Cheltenham Flyer'. To engine cleaners at Old Oak Common, the 'Castle' class meant a bigger boiler to clean, although they did have one advantage; the sand-boxes were situated underneath the footplate below the boiler, where the main steam-pipe entered the steam chest, thus there was much more room for fitters, cleaners and enginemen to work.

Later, in 1924, *Caerphilly Castle* was exhibited at the Wembley Exhibition and, during a visit to the exhibition, I paused to admire the engine. Six engine cleaners from Old Oak Common were constantly in attendance to keep the locomotive spick and span, these men having been picked specially for the job. For the first time, I realised how our work must look to the public, and it gave me a thrill to think of it. As a result of standing next to an LNER Pacific at Wembley, the 'Castle' sporting a notice which proclaimed it to be the 'most powerful locomotive in Britain', a series of exchanges between the two railways was organised for 1925. As locomotive cleaners, we became intensely interested in these trials, although our only

13

connection with them was that we were told to clean the 'foreigner', Gresley Class A1 Pacific No. 4474, later named *Victor Wild*. Of course, we did our best to clean the Pacific as we would our own engines, although it was strange cleaning an engine that had three cylinders rather than two or four.

One of the sights of the 1920s, before locomotive spotting reached anywhere near the proportions of the present day, was the line-up of locomotives at Old Oak Common on Cup Final day. It really was an astonishing sight to see every corner of the shed taken up with locomotives that had arrived, it would seem, from all parts of the GWR. It was extraordinary because the majority of the locomotives, which came to Old Oak Common on these football specials, were never seen in the London Division at any other time. They were mainly of the 'Star' and 'Saint' classes, although here and there a 47XX mixed traffic 2-8-0 or a Mogul would have been pressed into service. The carriage sidings, although never really devoid of passenger stock would, when viewed from Old Oak Lane, be a sea of gleaming chocolate and cream. How remarkable that although football specials are still run, this coming together of locomotives and carriages is very much a thing of the past.

It was possible to bring a locomotive from Paddington straight into Old Oak Common Shed, with the 'up' (overbridge) and 'down' carriage roads working very well until Old Oak Common East was reached. Here the passenger shunters were sometimes very short of space, especially on Cup Final day when the overflow of locomotives was put into the passenger sidings. These engines could not be cleaned here, nor could they be prepared for their return journeys, so a big organisation was involved getting them into the shed, at the appropriate time, for their return journey. Sometimes their boiler pressure had dropped so low that it was necessary to pull them in, which meant further trouble.

It was in 1924 that I was involved in my first strike, to which my immediate reaction was one of alarm. However, I soon realised that when a body of men are well organised and had a just cause, it was difficult, if not impossible, for employers to victimize individuals. I was involved in several strikes, none of which need concern us here except to say that the General Strike of 1926 left the most bitterness, partly because it need never have happened.

It is well-known that the GWR's tart publicity, in connection with the exploits of the 'Castle' class, encouraged a 'power competition' and the building of the Southern Railway 'Lord Nelson' and the LMS 'Royal Scot' classes. Going full circle, this inspired our General Manager, Sir Felix Pole, to retaliate with an even bigger engine and this was, of course, the famous 'King' class. Perhaps *King George V's* 'finest hour' was at the centenary celebrations of the Baltimore & Ohio Railway, where it so impressed the Americans that they presented it with a brass bell and medals, which have been carried by the locomotive ever since. It was a period of progress, and the 'King' class surely gave the GWR men something to be proud of.

I have always felt that *King George V* was the nearest thing to the *The Great Bear* in appearance, that I remember, as Mr Collett had clearly followed Churchward's clean lines of boiler and framing. The deep copper band which encircled the chimney, the brass safety-valve bonnet and the brass whistles, name and numberplates were all standard fittings on GWR passenger engines, but the larger boilers of the 'King' class locomotives seemed to make them, after polishing, stand out like a piece of jewellery in a glass cabinet.

This reminds me that, in direct contrast to other routes, the West of England line, that of the 'Cornish Riviera', express was particularly noted among engine cleaners for the condition of the engines on their return to Old Oak Common. Through Teignmouth and Dawlish the track is very close to the sea wall, and with a roughish sea and waves coming over the top, the spray would give the brasswork a dull salty look. Many are the times that I can remember 'King' class engines and others returning to Old Oak Common in this condition with a dirty boiler, the names and numberplates weather-beaten and almost black, and with wheels and outside motion filthy. Polishing up the brasswork of engines with short names like *Lode Star* was not too bad a task, but the reader can imagine for himself the work involved in cleaning names like *Knight of the Golden Fleece* or *Isambard Kingdom Brunel.* However, with our GWR 'pride in the job', we had them back at Paddington gleaming as if destined for a museum.

By the time that the last of the 'Kings' were appearing, I was a fairly senior engine cleaner and indeed, it was really unheard of for a man to spend seven or eight years in this grade. The age limit for promotion from cleaner to fireman was 25, but the GWR was compelled to rescind this rule, as many of their engine cleaners were now reaching this age while some were well past it. The position was that a cleaner had to be the oldest man in his grade before he was called to Swindon for promotion examinations; therefore, with less trains being run because of the industrial recession, promotion in any grade was almost non-existent. The position was made worse because drivers and firemen were being demoted to the lower grade, and were blocking our chances of advancement. Since this was swelling the numbers of engine cleaners, to a point which was considered undesirable and unnecessary, there was a serious suggestion that we should look for employment elsewhere. What chance was there with 2,750,000 unemployed? However, in praise of the Management, it could be said that in their eyes, once a driver, always a driver, and that although these men were put back, their wages were not affected. Perhaps this explains why the Great Western Railway, which was perhaps the most anti-socialist of railways, enjoyed such loyalty from employees who, to a man, were probably Labour voters!

In fact, it was to be nearly ten years before I had a chance to try my hand at firing, by which time I was a married man. Despite all the difficulties, I had decided that to wait until I was financially well off before getting married would virtually delay this event indefinitely. Since we were both working I decided that we should wait no longer and, in October 1932, I married Elizabeth Scurr, a Londoner, like myself. At the outset, there were some problems with my family, but these were soon smoothed over and we have always been very happy. To complete this part of the story, we eventually had three boys, born in 1936, 1943 and 1949, now all married with children of their own. None of them showed any desire to work on the railway although the second, Les, who is a teacher, has, without any encouragement from me, become very interested in railways, and has contributed articles to the railway magazines.

CHAPTER TWO

I had been engine cleaning for nearly ten years, and apart from a ride on the footplate of *The Great Bear*, I had managed only one previous footplate experience, when Driver Flaxman had taken me on to the footplate of a 'Dean Goods' engine. We had gone from the shed to the goods yard where he picked up his freight train and we proceeded from there to South Lambeth Goods Depot by way of Kensington and Chelsea. I remember glimpsing Battersea locomotive depot off to our right as we crossed the Southern line into Victoria. It was on this trip, while watching Driver Flaxman's fireman at work, that I began to pick up the art (and an art it was) of firing.

During the summer service of 1933, the exciting moment arrived. I was on the midday shift and 'Teddie' Tucker, our chargehand, called us out from the cleaners' cabin. In his hand he held a list of names from which he read 'Goldsworthy, Sawyer and Summers; report to the Running Foreman for firing duties'. For the three of us it was an exciting and tense moment, as it was our first turn of duty as firemen. Although this was only temporary promotion, it was what we had waited years to achieve.

During my years of cleaning at Old Oak Common, I had familiarised myself with practically the whole of a fireman's duties regarding the preparation of a locomotive so that my driver — regrettably I cannot now recall his name — had very little to tell me as far as shed duties were concerned. This first job was only a coach shunting turn in Old Oak Common passenger yard, but I thoroughly enjoyed the experience. More firing turns came my way during that summer, but in the winter, it was back to cleaning again.

The months went by, and although there were no more demotions, nor were there any cleaners made firemen, it seemed that the only reason for the absence of demotions was that there had been several retirements at Old Oak Common, leaving sufficient vacancies for all the men to maintain their grades. Then, early in 1934, there were rumours that the GWR were considering retiring their drivers at the age of 60 instead of 65 and, almost immediately, the senior firemen and cleaners began to receive their promotion forms requiring them to report to Swindon for examination. It was on 12th December 1934 that I received my paper, which read as follows; 'Chief Mechanical Engineer's Department. Please travel to Swindon for examination on Wednesday 19th December 1934 and report to the Company's Representative at Park House, Church Place ...' It continued with directions from Swindon Station to Park House and a request to bring 5s. an entry fee to the GWR Enginemen & Firemen's Mutual Assurance, Sick & Superannuation Society.

Practically all cleaners, assembled at Park House for examination found it difficult to pay the 5s. as it was alot of money, but it was compulsory and refusal to join the MAS would have barred us from the footplate. Now that I have retired, I bless the GWR for their foresight, because without my MAS pension life would be very hard indeed. The sum of 5s. or 25p as it is now, does not seem a lot of money and, at today's prices, it certainly is not; but its value in 1934 can be judged from a GWR restaurant car menu card of 1937, which offered the following:

DINNER 5/-
TOMATO JUICE COCKTAIL
or
CONSOMME BRUNOISE

_ * _

BOILED SALMON HOLLANDAISE

_ * _

VOL-AU-VENT REGENCE

_ * _

ROAST LAMB & MINT SAUCE
GREEN PEAS   VEGETABLE MARROW
ROAST & BOILED POTATOES

COLD

ROAST CHICKEN   YORK HAM
ROAST BEEF   OX TONGUE

SALAD

CHERRY TART & CREAM
FRESH APRICOT MELBA
CHEESE AND BISCUITS
DESSERT

COFFEE per cup 4d. extra

* * * * * *

DINNER 3/6

SOUP

FISH OR JOINT of POULTRY

SWEETS or CHEESE

* * * * * *

Such a meal at today's prices would leave little or nothing out of £5. Indeed, a cup of British Railways coffee — instant, not ground as on GWR cars — cost the equivalent of the price for that whole dinner!

Anyway, this time there were no problems at Swindon, as not even the coloured wools for the eyesight test or the box of sand for flat feet held any perils; I was able to return to my wife with the news that I had passed for fireman. However, once again, my dreams were shattered. Just after Christmas I was called into the Running Foreman's office, and told that I had been appointed to Banbury Shed as a fireman! This was appalling news, but no appeal to the Foreman had any effect. However, whilst walking across the shed on the Thursday prior to my removal I saw Fred Woodruffe, our ASLEF Representative, and I mentioned the situation to him. Imagine my surprise when he immediately flared up and told me in no uncertain way, that he had not been told about this, that he was not going to have it and, in fact, he wanted seven more firemen at Old Oak Common before any man was transferred. He did not bother with the Foreman but put through a telephone call straight to Swindon and, shortly afterwards, my transfer was rescinded!

I spent very little time on shunting duties before being promoted to local train work, which involved firing duties on such engines as the 6100 class 2-6-2Ts, Moguls and 5700 class pannier tanks. There were also turns on empty stock workings, running between Old Oak Common passenger yard and Paddington, with engines of the 'Hall' class providing the power. Although a little scared of these at first — invariably they consisted of fifteen coaches, and were a very heavy pull on the carriage overbridge line into Paddington — they gave the feeling, running into the terminus, that at last you were 'someone to be noticed'. It was on these trips that we 'young' firemen began to exploit all we had learnt about firing a locomotive, and my first regular driver was a great encouragement in this.

Charlie Brown was the man in question, and his first words to me were to enquire whether I was in the Union, and then what I knew technically about the locomotive. My answer to the last question being 'nothing', he said, 'You will know a lot more than nothing when you leave me'. Being a young fireman at this time, I had little actual interest in matters technical but as the weeks passed, at every available opportunity Charlie would get out the GWR Rule Book, or technical books about GWR locomotives, and I began to find that despite my reluctance to learn, I was taking it in and building up a store of knowledge.

Charlie was a first class engineman, and knew practically every rule in the book by its number. His knowledge of different valve gear arrangements was astonishing. I was amazed, and suddenly realised that he was trying to pass on this information for my own ultimate benefit. I became Charlie's willing pupil, constantly listening and remembering. I should mention that Charlie Brown's value was later recognised by the GWR, in that he was appointed to the position of London Division Locomotive Running Inspector. He also served the GWR in another way, as a local councillor, helping, amongst other things, to get a supply of purer town water for use in the water-columns.

As some evidence of his great knowledge of the rule book, I remember booking on early one morning for a shunting turn with him; I got up on to the engine, a 5700 class pannier tank, to examine the fire, while Charlie walked round the locomotive and the attached shunting truck. He noticed that the truck had a shackle coupling on, and when the shunters appeared, he asked them to put the screw on. Their reaction was to the effect that if he wanted it done he could do it 'his self'. Charlie sat fast and refused to move; 6.30 became 7.30 and then 9.30 so the shunters rang Paddington, and the authorities there rang Old Oak Common to enquire who the driver was on the shunting turn. Eventually Charlie was called to the phone, and asked to explain himself. This he did, pointing out that the rule book stated that when shunting was taking place in residential areas, a screw coupling had to be fitted. Charlie's persistence was rewarded, as this was the rule. After this kind of tuition I could hardly go wrong and although I passed on to other and more interesting work, I always remained indebted to Charlie for that early guidance.

In what was known as the West London link, which consisted of passenger and freight train workings, my driver was Ike Pollicutt, a massive man who was all brawn and muscle but, at the same time, very easy going and thoroughly likeable. It was said that when he was passenger fireman himself, in the days when train crews had their 'own' engine, he spent practically all his money in the 'Kenilworth Castle' public house, near where he lived in Kenilworth Road, and an amazing but true coincidence was that he did a lot of his firing on No. 4097 *Kenilworth Castle!* Some of these trains in the West London link were freight turns to West Norwood or Hither Green marshalling yards, worked mainly by Class 5700 engines. Passenger work consisted of trains to Aylesbury, High Wycombe, Windsor, and on what we would now call commuter trains, with very short stops at stations. It always seemed to me that when working on these jobs, we were always in a great hurry.

After about two years, I came on to a more interesting type of job although, by work standards, it was still a long way from main line express work. This was preparing a 2800 class 2-8-0 locomotive, and working a South Wales empty coal train as far as Swindon or Reading. Here we would be relieved by other men, who worked the train forward while we brought their train, usually loaded with coal, back to Acton, Paddington or Old Oak Common goods. Although the maximum speed of these trains would only be about 25 to 30m.p.h., they were very heavy and the driver needed a full head of steam to keep going. The 2800 class of engine, built for pulling power and not for speed, was unbeatable at this sort of work, yet the know-how of keeping plenty of steam for the driver while, at the same time, making sure that the water was always at a safe level in the boiler, could only be learnt by at first making numerous errors. Even so, it is fair to say that whatever sort of mess you made of it, these engines rarely jibbed at poor firing, and never let us down.

There was still a need for instruction to be given to firemen so drivers would, whenever possible, give the benefit of their experience to their fireman, but on this type of work, they were usually fully occupied. With a heavy train of loose-coupled coal wagons, and with only the engine's brakes to bring it to a stand without breaking the couplings or shaking up the guard, there was little time for the driver to instruct his fireman. Sometimes we would be brought to a stand with the signals against us, and the driver would then pick up the shovel and show you how to put the coal on the fire in the right quantity and sequence.

After firing the 2800 class engines, on jobs such as these South Wales coal trains, a fireman would have gained valuable knowledge of the long fireboxes, so his introduction to the 'Hall' class on passenger work would, while being a lot more arduous, be taken in his stride. A good driver could make a fireman's job a lot easier by nursing the engine although, in later years, such were the loads put behind the engines that the driver needed the full co-operation of his fireman to maintain schedules. This, of course, all started back at the shed with the making up of the fire.

I would use the long rake (about 12ft. in length) to spread the existing fire over the firebars. Then, after climbing on to the tender, I would break up about a ton and a half of coal into reasonable lumps and then throw it into the firebox, by hand, to build up the fire. While I was attending to my other duties the coal would ignite and build up into a considerable furnace, to which I could add smaller coal with the shovel, building it up from the firebox doors to about half-way down the box. I would now have a black mound of coal near the mouth, but half-way down the firebox to the tube plate, the fire would be glowing bright red just where the terrific heat was required to make steam. Before cleaning up the footplate, I would put more coal on the fire. The box would be nearly three-quarters full, but the slope from the firehole door was still visible. I often contemplated the fact, while preparing an engine on shed that, once on the road, I should be throwing every shovelful nearly 10ft!

At Paddington we would back down on to our train, which was usually ten or twelve coaches in length. The fire was now 'quiet', and when the driver received the 'right away' from the guard, and as soon as the engine was clear of the station canopy, I would get the long rake from the fire rack, which was at my side of the cab, and begin to stir up the fire all over the box. Passing Old Oak Common, I would begin to shovel coal into the firebox, throwing it from the shovel over the now red mound at the firehole doors, so that the blast would take it down to the tube plate and therefore maintain a constant pressure. Here, experience began to count; the front end of the firebox had to be fed constantly, but should I use too much and block the tube plate then steam pressure would begin to drop immediately. Thus the successful method we learnt, from making mistakes, was to frequently fire into the four corners of the box, and along the sides and front end.

During those first months firing on the 2800 class locomotives, I began to get a whole new experience of life from the places through which we passed on the GWR. Only rarely had I previously left the built-up areas, along the back of which the railway ran for miles in the suburbs of London, and gone out into the country. Places such as Maidenhead, High Wycombe, Slough and Greenford, the extent of trips on short distance passenger trains, were just local work while the interesting, if harder work, was yet to come. This was hinted at by the first holiday that we were able to take, in September 1937.

The journey from Paddington to the West Country, after passing Southall and the industrial area towards Slough was, to the lover of the countryside, very beautiful. A person brought up in and used only to London's streets could be excused if he began to think that he was entering a new world. On a clear day it was possible, when sitting on the 'down' side of the line as you approached Langley, to see the stately pile of Windsor Castle in the far distance. When working a train from Paddington to Windsor the driver always looked, as he approached Windsor Station, to see if the Royal Standard was flying over the castle. This meant that the King was in residence, and woe betide any driver who allowed smoke to issue from the chimney of his locomotive whilst at Windsor. This was indeed a serious offence, although co-operation between driver and fireman usually avoided this happening.

The panorama of the Downs and the Chiltern Hills was always in view when approaching Reading, where we stopped for a couple of minutes before we were off again on our journey to the west, down Brunel's original main line. Today, most West of England trains go over the Berks & Hants line from Paddington but then it was, perhaps because of tradition, more obvious to go via Bristol.

Didcot, shortly to feature very greatly in my life, was our next passing place after which we reached Wantage Road where *Jane*, the old tramway engine, was still at work trundling trucks of coal along the road to Wantage Town. Then, after the stop at Swindon, we passed the Works, the home of GWR locomotives and indeed, most things 'Great Western'. For many years, it was possible to see here siding after siding of locomotives, resplendent in their magnificent GWR livery all awaiting departure to their home depot to re-enter service.

At Bristol, I got out to go to the station buffet for some tea, also spending time to see if any Old Oak Common men were on our engine. I was disappointed, as they had just been changed over, but I noticed that the engine was No. 4022, once named *King William* but now *Belgian Monarch* so as not to confuse the observer with the altogether more important 'King' class. This reminds me that at Old Oak Common, we had private wagers about the names of GWR locomotives; for example, which was the longest and so on. At Old Oak Common we would see, at some time or another, most of the big passenger engines, and be able to answer these questions at first hand. I can still remember many of them and can easily recall, simply because Frank Burridge once told me to clean its brasswork, that No. 4016 *Knight of the Golden Fleece* was the longest name on the GWR. As I have said before, the reader can imagine polishing those letters up!

I never actually worked beyond Bristol down to Devon where that holiday was taken, but the journey was a percursor to many made on the footplate to places all over the GWR, and later on other railways as well.

There was one firing job which gave us our first introduction to driving. On arrival at Old Oak Common Shed, a locomotive was left by the driver on the coal stage road where other drivers, mainly men whose eyesight was not strong enough for main line trains, would continually close these engines up together (for them to take on coal), thereby leaving a space for other engines arriving on shed to be left in the same place. Also working on this road were the fire droppers; some clearing the dead fires from fireboxes while others removed the ash from smokeboxes and boiler tubes. Sometimes there was animosity between these grades as the engine driver was in no hurry, but the fire dropper and tube runner, who were not qualified to move engines, were on piece work. Therefore the coal stage road became blocked, no more engines could get into the shed, except via the ash pit and, in this case, the piece-work men's earnings slumped!

Really, it paid drivers to get on with the job before the engine went cold, and boiler pressure became too low to move it into the shed. It was on this shed duty that we became acquainted with all the classes of GWR engine, with most drivers allowing their firemen to take engines from the coal stage into the shed on their own. This was really forbidden, of course, but, as we have seen, the movement of engines had to be continual and indeed, it would cause delay to engines getting to Paddington to work their trains. In these circumstances, providing that the shed driver thought the fireman was capable of driving engines, it enabled the work to run more smoothly. Of course, he took full responsibility.

We did, in fact, receive unofficial driving instruction on various engines from our drivers, whenever possible, on turns of duty where time to do so was available. I had always been interested in watching my drivers at work so the knowledge which I had acquired was now put to good use, but it must be remembered that very great care had to be exercised when moving engines from the coal stage as sometimes, after the fire had been drawn, steam pressure would be very low and, consequently, brake pressure would be much weaker. Therefore, stopping the locomotive often had to be done by means of the handbrake.

As an illustration, I will explain that which I thought to be the most difficult procedure. When the engine came off the shed turntable, the man driving had to remember that the pit roads had, at their end, a steel box about 6in. high. To touch this with the locomotive at too great a speed would bring it off the rails, so you will, no doubt, readily see that, with low steam pressure, you had to have enough speed to get off the turntable, and stop gently against the stops by means of the tender brake.

Sometimes the most experienced of drivers got into trouble with the engine jumping the stops but, considering all the facts, the Management at subsequent enquiries were usually very lenient, and the driver's punishment was a verbal caution. In cases where no reasonable exceptions could be considered, the punishment was more severe, usually involving suspension and a registered caution which was virtually a black mark to remain on one's record for ever.

Right: Park House, Swindon, built by the GWR and used for many years as an examination centre for its employees.
L. A. Summers

Below: *City of Truro* in 1957 at Southampton Terminus after the author had worked the 12.44 from Didcot.
A. W. Summers Collection

CHAPTER THREE

It was in 1937 that the Great Western Railway introduced a new express train, the 'Bristolian', which was to make the 117.65 mile journey from Paddington to Bristol in 105 minutes. This train was at first hauled by locomotives of the 'King' class, but the Running Department soon realised that the 'Castle' class locomotives were equally capable of working the train. Therefore, they soon took it over, and provided motive power for the 'Bristolian' until 1958 when the diesel-hydraulics were used. The 'Bristolian' became world famous and, for many years, was the fastest booked start to stop timing on a British railway. It added great lustre to the already spectacular names of Old Oak Common drivers. These main line express passenger drivers were in an absolute class of their own, as there was no one who was their equal; there is no doubt that they were, to use a modern phrase, 'the greatest'. Many years of experience had put them on a pedestal, although if some of the headboards from these men's trains had been removed, they would have descended to the equality of all drivers!

In the heyday of the GWR, driving such trains as the 'Bristolian', the 'Cheltenham Flyer' or the 'Cornish Riviera' was to be part of a legend, although the tip of the mountain was achieved upon driving the Royal Train. With Windsor Castle being located on the Great Western lines, King George V and Queen Mary, when travelling on the GWR in the Royal Train, were always drawn by 'Castle' Class No. 4082 *Windsor Castle*. I have seen at first hand how this machine was prepared by the mechanical staff — to sum it up, it seemed sometimes that No. 4082 would be almost dismantled and rebuilt! To be entrusted to drive the engine on such a train was the pinnacle of achievement.

All these now legendary drivers had differing characteristics; some would delight in harassing the fitters in order to get every insignificant little repair done to their engine, while some were non-union men which, despite their obvious ability as drivers, put them at a disadvantage to the great body of men who were. I particularly remember a driver named George Bailey who, to engine cleaners, was a horror. It did not matter how clean his engine was because he would always find something wrong, and such was his complaining nature, that if possible we always cleaned it under the supervision of the chargehand cleaner. However, this man had a heart of gold. I remember when one of the engine cleaners slipped and fell into an engine pit, supposedly through losing his balance due to oil on the pit sides, he was off sick for some time. We arranged, with the Running Foreman, to have a pay day collection for him as he was married with three children, this being the usual practice where a man had been off sick for a period of time, provided that he was a union member, of course.

About half a dozen collectors, each for a period of two hours, would wait by the pay office with a box, and collect the voluntary subscriptions. The average contribution was about 2s. 6d., and no one refused, whether they be cleaner, fireman or driver. I was at the pay window myself when George Bailey came across to draw his money. He put 5s. in my box, which was an extremely generous gesture indeed, which somehow seemed out of character for the martinet who was never satisfied.

Anyway, enough has been written by others, about the famous named trains of the Great Western Railway, for me to pass over them without repeating what is already well-known. Indeed, the racing days were soon to come to an end when the long feared, but almost inevitable war finally came about, in September 1939. To me, after overcoming considerable deprivation to have a good job with prospects, and now enjoying life to the full, it seemed as though the cycle was changing back to the horror of the past. We knew that this time, with science's devilish contraptions, it was going to be even more destructive, and that the railways would become an essential part of the military strategy and a legitimate target for the enemy.

The GWR, like all the railway companies, was taken over by the Government immediately war was declared, and it soon became a common sight to see all kinds of unusual locomotives in the London area, working on jobs previously the preserve of some other type of engine. For instance, the 5700 class 0-6-0 condensing tanks, Nos. 9700-9710, had always been used exclusively for conveying meat, in refrigerated containers, from Acton Yard to Paddington suburban, and thence to Smithfield Meat Market via the underground lines. These engines had a pipe from the smokebox to the water tank and the fireman, by operating a lever at his side known as the 'chopper', could condense the smoke and exhaust steam in the water tank, thus ensuring that no smoke was emitted into the Underground tunnels. As some indication of the exclusivness of their use on these jobs, I remember that, after I had moved to Didcot, I was preparing my locomotive on an outside pit when I heard Driver Bill White, in rather forceful terms, demand of his fireman, who was standing on top of one of these locomotives with the bag of the water-column in the tank, how much more 'ruddy water' it wanted before it was full. Meekly, the fireman replied that it was just over a foot from the top of the tank.

From where I was, I could see that water was pouring from the tank overflow pipe, which indicated to me that, on this particular type of engine, the tanks were full. Now, no man in his right mind would question anything which Bill White did; he was a passenger train driver, and knew all the answers. Yet it was apparent to me that he did not know the answer to the present dilemma. The question was, was I bold enough to tell him, because evidently his fireman did not know either. It transpired that this locomotive had been on its way from Swindon Works back to Old Oak Common, but as the Swindon men had not known the road beyond Didcot, and with nobody being on hand to relieve them on the station, they had brought it into Didcot locomotive depot. Bill White, booking on duty later, had been assigned to take it light engine to Old Oak Common.

Now, I knew that it was not possible to fill the water tank right up to the top on these locomotives, as a space was left above the water level to condense the smoke from the boiler when working on the London Transport underground lines to Smithfield. It was apparent that Bill White did not know anything about the 'chopper', or the pump which was fitted in preference to the normal injectors, and which could not be used on the electrified lines. Therefore, I decided that perhaps I ought to explain all this to him, so with much trepidation I approached him. I have always thought that he did not really believe me but, knowing that I originated from Old Oak Common myself, he probably accepted it, having in his mind the thought that if I was wrong which, of course, I was not, he could heap the consequences on me!

These condensing locomotives were now appearing on other work, to release more suitable engines for heavier traffic. Another rare sight in the London Division were the Aberdare double-framed 2-6-0s, used entirely on freight working and which usually remained in the South Wales area. These engines, which some claim to have been the worst ever built by the GWR, were now working through to Acton Yard. During my firing years, I had seen this class of engine only rarely but now, when we were called upon to work a train from Swindon to Acton Yard, it became increasingly common to find one of these at its head. When we took charge there was often very little coal left in the tender, and the fire had become very dirty. Coal trains were now given little preference on the main lines, and we were often turned on to loops to allow Government munitions or sometimes troop trains to pass. Also, more and more passenger trains were being cancelled, with the locomotives being used for essential workings such as these.

Drivers and firemen on the railway had been exempt from joining the forces, as it was felt that their specialised experience of train working could be best utilised by them remaining at their jobs. Those employed in shipbuilding and other industries, vital to the war effort, were similarly classified, but problems arose with the appearance of young men in civilian clothes likely to provoke mothers whose own sons had been conscripted into the forces. Therefore it became necessary to issue railwaymen with a badge for identification but even so, it became a common sight on the railways to see women guards, ticket collectors and so on; almost every grade was included, even permanent way workers.

Of course, Old Oak Common and Willesden (LMS) sheds, as well as the Park Royal Industrial Estate, were all important targets for Hitler's bombers, but while the LMS installations received direct hits on several occasions, Old Oak Common seemed to have a charmed life, probably because of the anti-aircraft batteries which were situated quite close by on Wormwood Scrubs. As we shall see, this immunity came to a rather spectacular end.

The glass roof of the shed had, of course, been blacked over, but we were still compelled to have the engine black out sheets down all round when preparing a locomotive for the road. This prevented the reflection of the flames, when the firehole door was opened, from being seen from the air. Putting coal on the fire, and carrying out other duties of a fireman in these conditions was very difficult; even when the cold winter weather was upon us, engine crews would sweat in the humid temperature under these sheets until it became almost too much to bear.

In these black-out conditions, taking water at the columns in winter was a miserable job. The water that had dripped from the bag after the previous use would freeze round the column and, because it could not be seen in the darkness you very often slipped over on it and many times the air raid sirens would wail to add to your discomfort. When this happened we were inclined to go to the air raid shelters, until we realised that this was a great help to Hitler and just what he would like to happen, because once the railway ceased to run, Britain would come to a halt. We knew that the main targets of the Luftwaffe would be locomotive sheds and freight yards, but this was our war effort and, although we were in a reserved occupation, this really was the front line as much as any in France.

There were other, perhaps less expected aspects of these air attacks. Like most railwaymen I walked to work and often I would stand still in Tubbs Road, or outside Willesden Junction Station, on the way to Old Oak Common and listen to a bomb whistling down,

30

feeling quite sure by the sound of it, that it was coming straight for me. I remember on one occassion, when on night duty, I walked down Tubbs Road with an LMS signalman who was also going on duty. I heard later that his box had been blown to pieces, no trace of him was ever found.

Engine crews had been issued with gas masks and steel helmets, which were required to be carried at all times although really, we did not need orders to carry them. During air raids shrapnel was always falling around like rain and I remember, only too vividly, two occasions when I had to dive for cover as low flying enemy aircraft machine gunned the shed as I was walking towards the coal stage.

Another typical incident, out on the line, concerned a Government stores train that we were working up from Wolverhampton. It had been a nightmare journey all the way, especially through the industrial area of Birmingham, and as we approached Snow Hill Tunnel we felt sure that we were never going to get through. As far as lighting the streets was concerned, Birmingham should have been completely blacked out, but the power of the flares and incendiary bombs dropped by the German planes, despite the terrific hammering they were getting from the anti-aircraft guns, lit up everything as if it were daylight.

Coming out of Snow Hill Tunnel we quickly took in our signals, which were all at 'line clear'. My driver and I breathed a sigh of relief because at last, it seemed that we could still keep going. Once through Tyseley we began to leave the factory area behind, but on both sides of the line, bombs that were undoubtedly meant for the railway were falling everywhere. Fortunately we had a very free steaming 'Hall', and despite the fact that my driver and I were working completely covered in by the black-out sheets I was able to keep a full head of steam.

Solihull was quickly passed, and approaching Lapworth, all that could be heard was the bark of the engine's exhaust. After passing through Hatton and Warwick we swept round the bend which brought us into Leamington, where we knew we would be stopped if, for any reason, we could not proceed. Here we stopped to take water, and took the opportunity to ask the station staff about the situation ahead. We were informed that everything was quiet as far as Oxford.

We were soon under way again, and after passing Fenny Compton my driver shut off steam. I shut the firehole doors, and took down the black-out sheets to get a welcome breath of fresh air. From here, we could maintain speed on to Banbury without additional coal being required on the fire. At Banbury, it was possible to hear but not see shunting in progress, while faint glimmers of light were visible from beneath engines standing in the shed. Oxford was passed without incident as was Didcot, but at Reading we were stopped at the West Junction signal box and told by the signalman that we had an 'Air Raid Red' — code words which meant that the bombing of London was again in progress. We needed no telling for in the distance the sky was on fire.

These 'Air Raid Red' warnings were, of course, quite common, being a nightly occurrence. On another occasion, with a 6300 class 2-6-0, we received the usual warnings and by Slough, the bombing and gunfire could be heard plainly. From West Drayton we were being continually stopped by signals and we were informed that we were going to be turned into Hanwell Bridge Siding, because of the congestion of trains ahead. The driver brought the train to a stand clear of the main line at the stop signal close to Hanwell Viaduct — itself a favourite target for Hitler's bombers. The signals and points controlling the outlet from these sidings were operated by a shunter signalman, but he was nowhere to be seen. My driver could not get through to Control on the telephone, to find whether the train was to be left there, and when I walked back to the guard's van, he also was gone!

Our position then, in the middle of the night and with an air raid raging around us, was that we had been diverted off the main line into these sidings to await further orders, but we could not contact anyone, and no one seemed to want to concern themselves with us!

The Moguls offered very little in the way of overhead protection, because the cab roof was shorter than that fitted to the 4-6-0 classes. The noise of exploding bombs was very close and we were a sitting target for any bomber, unable to lift a finger in our own defence. I suppose we could have abandoned the train, but that seemed like desertion and, in fact, had we left it, there was nowhere we could have gone which was any safer than where we were. Therefore we remained, listening to the bombs whistling down and the shrapnel rattling on the cab roof, watching flames light up the sky and wondering if we should ever reach home.

It was a night I shall never forget. When I finally got home, I had been on duty for over 24 hours. It was, of course, a very worrying time for all train crews working away from home, with the thought in mind of 'would your house and family still be there when you returned?'

During October 1940, the marshalling yards in the London area experienced an 'alert' almost every night, with the result that out of 382 hours of darkness, shunting had to be carried out in complete darkness for 299 hours. Although my fireman's duties did not take me on shunting turns, I would be on turns that brought trains into Old Oak Common Yard.

One day I was returning with my driver on a 5700 class pannier tank and a train of loaded box vans from South Lambeth. We had just crossed the LMS line at North Pole Junction on to our own line, and had proceeded alongside the 'down' main line to the reception line in the shunting sidings, where we came to a halt. I remember thinking that it was very quiet; the guns on the 'Scrubs' were silent, the clock on the Carriage Department offices said 1.23p.m., my driver was making some entries in his daily record and shunting was in progress around us. Then, slowly but plainly, the noise of Spitfire engines could be heard coming closer. This was a familiar and friendly sort of noise, so we paid no attention to it.

Then, right behind me it seemed, the unmistakable whistling noise was heard. There was no time to move or to do anything but listen. Almost at once there was a terrific explosion and I swear that the engine on my side rose off the rails. One after another came more bombs, accompanied each time by a huge explosion. About eight bombs in all were dropped, and to this day I am sure that the second, which exploded behind the engine and left a huge crater in the track, lifted our locomotive back on to the rails!

The third somehow missed all the main lines, but hit the roof of the Carriage Department offices. The clock stopped at 1.25p.m. and remained at that time for some years afterwards! Had that building been hit 25 minutes later, about sixty of the staff of the carriage sidings would have been in their cabins, changing out of their overalls to go off duty. There is no doubt that all of them would have been killed, but as it was, the only casualty was a burst water main, which caused considerable havoc itself with flooding.

The fourth bomb hit the locomotive paint shop and demolished it, while the sixth, seventh and eighth, no doubt intended for the locomotive shed, all missed. One narrowly missed the Grand Junction Canal wall, which ran alongside the shed and had this been breached, hundreds of tons of water would have poured into the shed. All this took place in a very short space of time, during which not one anti-aircraft gun fired a shot. Like everyone else, the gunners were taken completely by surprise, being misled by the sound of the aircraft engines. We learned later that the Spitfires had been captured by the Germans. Considerable havoc was caused, but I was extremely worried because although most of the bombs had missed their real targets, I was concerned that they might have fallen in nearby All Souls Avenue where my wife was at the time. Fortunately, everything at home was all right.

However, the strain of events like these was terrific. My wife, sleeping daily in tube stations with hundreds of others, in particular was noticing its effect. After Christmas 1940, I decided to apply for a transfer to Didcot locomotive shed, a small shed seventeen miles beyond Reading. I was not alone in this decision — many of the drivers and firemen at Old Oak Common decided to transfer mainly, it should be stressed, for our own peace of mind regarding our families. Although we should still be exposed to the dangers of aerial bombardment, it would be something to know that our wives and children were safe.

Locomotive men must have been urgently required at Didcot because, about a week later, I was called into the foreman's office and told that my transfer had been accepted. Indeed, this went through so quickly that it was a couple of weeks before I could get my wife and son down with me. Thus came to an end eighteen years at the top shed on the Great Western Railway, eighteen very happy years with the best of workmates.

CHAPTER FOUR

All railway enthusiasts know of Didcot, the headquarters of the Great Western Society, so it may surprise them to know that previous to the 1960s, Didcot was one of those places, and there are others, which were vital to the economy of the country, but which remained unnoticed by cartographers and journalists. Look at a map of the South Midlands, dating from only twenty years ago, and you will find the railway junction marked, but there is either no name to it or a code description out of all proportion to the facts, although Wallingford, Wantage and other less important places would be marked.

In fact, Didcot was largely created by the Great Western Railway, when the latter made it the point of junction between the original main line, and what became a line through Oxford to Birmingham and the north. The first station at Didcot consisted of narrow platforms under an all-over roof of timber packed with pitch. This was a fatal combination because, in 1886, a porter attending to oil lamps in the waiting-room negligently spilt some of this oil, splashing it across the waiting-room fire. The great heat burning in the chimney, as a result of this oil, became too much; the flames ignited the flue, and jumped through into the telegraph office. With the roof alight, the flames soon engulfed the whole station. Great fires were common in the 19th century, but this must have been a fire amongst fires because a notice-board, 20 yards from the station, burst into flames as a result of the heat.

Afterwards, a new station was built and, with a number of enlargements, it still serves the Western Region's HSTs at the present time. The original junction was augmented in 1882, with the opening of the Didcot, Newbury & Southampton Railway and with several local branches, this provided a great deal of locomotive work. During World War I, an Army Ordnance Depot was established to the west of the station which, together with what was known as Milton Depot, an RAF establishment, eventually covered a vast area with 77 miles of railway track.

The first shed at Didcot, for the broad gauge, had been built when the Oxford branch was under construction in 1844. Until the completion of the Birmingham line, in 1852, it housed the engines which worked this line but, thereafter, had no regular allocation. Then, in 1856, the mixed gauge was extended southwards through Didcot to Basingstoke, and a new brick and timber mixed gauge shed was built opposite what is now platform 5, just to the east of the existing shunters' hut. Obviously as other branches were built, particularly the Newbury and Southampton lines, the need for a shed increased, although its allocation in the 1920s was only about thirty engines. Most of these were double-framed 4-4-0s or 0-6-0s of various vintages. Among the 4-4-0s were engines like 'Duke' class No. 3255 *Excalibur*, various nameless 'Bulldog' class locomotives, the occasional 'Flower' or 'County' and even, at one time, one of the strange reversed 0-4-4T 4-4-0s, No. 3551.

While the broad gauge shed, built at Oxford in 1854, continued to do business until after steam came to an end, Didcot's veteran shed was replaced in 1932 by the four road building which still stands, and houses the engines of the Great Western Society. This is, of course, the shed with which I am familiar. It was a standard structure, not only used in other locations but for non-railway jobs as well. Like Old Oak Common, these structures were provided with connections on the roof beams, to ease the job of adding additional sections should that become necessary which, with Didcot, was never the case.

Didcot's allocation of engines stood at about fifty in 1950, and remained at around that figure until the Newbury branch was closed. Among these locomotives were the three 2251 class 0-6-0s, Nos. 3210, 3211 and 3212, sent new to Didcot in the last month of 1947. They remained on the strength until the closure of the Newbury to Winchester line in 1960. After this, they passed to other locations but, within four years, all three had been withdrawn, having spent the greater part of their incredibly short lives on Didcot's allocation list of engines. There were also some Austerity 2-8-0s, but the less said about these, the better.

One of the GWR Simplex petrol shunters was also on the strength of Didcot Shed for many years, although we did not see very much of it. It worked exclusively in the Provender Store, and was always kept over there when not in use. I remember that, for a long time, its driver was an 'eyesight man' named Rickard.

When, during the war, I first came to Didcot, I could never understand why this establishment was not a target for aerial bombardment. Perhaps a clue was provided by two separate incidents. One evening, I was on duty at 10.15p.m. and, whilst preparing an LMS 'Black Five' the sirens sounded. To me the reaction of the staff at the shed was, to say the least, embarrassing. They immediately made for the shelters and before I had realised it, my driver had put down his oil feeder and was gone. Looking around I was tempted to make some defamatory remark about this but I refrained. I was no hero and anyway, their behaviour was wholly understandable in the circumstances.

The noise from the enemy planes could be heard very plainly but there was no anti-aircraft fire, no searchlights, nothing. Gradually the aircraft flew on to their destination, probably Birmingham or Coventry, and afterwards nothing could be heard but the gentle hiss of escaping steam, as the boiler pressure mounted on unattended locomotives. No bombs had been unleashed upon us and no flares had been dropped to light up the sky, which, in itself, was astonishing because there was no doubt that Didcot was an important railway junction.

On several occasions, bombs were dropped around Didcot but almost all fell on open countryside and were, I think, dropped by pilots who, in sheer desperation, were trying to lighten the load of a crippled plane. In one such incident an enemy plane, returning from a raid on some industrial town, was losing height as it approached Didcot, when the gunner of a light pom-pom, which had been installed on the Provender Store, fired upon it. Resulting from this, the gunner was court-martialled, for opening fire without receiving orders to do so! That gun, like a similar one in Moreton Cutting Yard, was intended for defence rather than attack and firing on the enemy would, of course, have drawn attention to the fact that there was something here to protect.

All classes of locomotive worked into the 'depot', as it was always known, but the larger machines were confined to the length of their train and exit to shed facilities. Normal services were worked by various 0-6-0PTs, in particular Nos. 907, 1861, 2784, 5752, 3622 and 3721, with three of them working 24 hours each day. They were provided with a unique GWR, but almost Yankee looking, spark arrester. Two passenger trains left every evening, taking depot workers to Oxford and Reading and returning with them each morning. These trains were usually worked by a 2251 class 0-6-0 or a 6100 class 2-6-2T. Didcot men allocated to shunting duties in the ordnance depot walked from the shed, to take over from the men who had completed their turn of duty.

By virtue of my seniority, I soon found that at Didcot I was on main line work, and this caused some upset among the locomotive men. Whilst not unfriendly, the local men were a little suspicious of men from Old Oak Common, whom they regarded as a kind of superior being and who, they believed, were inclined to look down on small sheds which, I suppose, was correct. It was, of course, the firemen who felt this most because they knew that, with my experience, I should soon be placed above quite a lot of them.

However, the locomotive men were being increased to double strength, and every week new faces appeared. Men from Devon and Cornwall, Wales, Wolverhampton and Old Oak Common were sent to Didcot, because it was feared that there would be losses among those working the trains from the ordnance depot to Southampton Docks. The home-bred Didcot men were outnumbered by these additions to the staff, and it was really amazing to be in the locomotive cabin and listen to the different accents.

More and more of these turns — through trains from the north to Southampton Docks — were being sent to Didcot, so much so that it became increasingly necessary to put leading firemen on to driving duties. Whilst this did not affect me immediately, the start of the annual leave period saw six drivers off duty each week and, consequently, six more firemen were 'booked out' on driving turns, and that included me. I had, during my career as a fireman, always assisted the driver with the observation of signals, which was part of my job anyway. Additionally my drivers, particularly at Old Oak Common, had taught me how to handle different locomotives, and I had picked up valuable experience of driving techniques with passenger and freight trains in this way. This was now very valuable knowledge, as it enabled me to take charge of all classes of main line train.

I well remember my first turn as an acting driver, on a coal train from Didcot Goods Yard to Newbury Yard hauled by 'Bulldog' class 4-4-0 No. 3408 *Bombay*. Fortunately I was given an efficient fireman, for it was no easy road to Newbury, via Compton. Being very experienced on this route as a fireman, I knew exactly what was required. The Didcot to Newbury line was a single track railway, with facilities for trains to pass at the stations. Now, with developments in progress for the invasion of Europe, more and more traffic was going over this route, so it was decided that the single line would have to be doubled. This entailed an almost complete remodelling of the line, although it was nowhere near the same kind of problem that it had been to its original engineers. Twelve drivers were required to work the special engineering trains which ran each day, and it was decided that the twelve leading firemen at Didcot should be promoted for driving duties on these trains. I was now the most senior fireman at Didcot and was, therefore, included in the list of twelve.

The path of these trains would be anywhere between Didcot and Winchester, depending solely on the class of materials being carried, and where it was being used. Sometimes it would be an empty ballast train from Didcot Yard to Upton or Compton, here a huge gap was being cut into the grassy bank to accommodate the extra track. Sometimes we went to Sutton Scotney, with a heavy train load of clinker or ash for ballast. As the work progressed, there would be rails, sleepers, bulk timber for bridges, and so on. Labour on this work was mainly provided by Irish labourers but there were, of course, the GWR's own permanent way gangs, as well as Engineers who were in charge of the more important work.

The majority of trains were very heavy, yet the motive power available was limited by the standard of the route. The usual motive power was 2251 class 0-6-0s or Moguls, but sometimes the old 'standbys' on this route, 'Bulldog' class No. 3408 *Bombay* or No. 3448 *Kingfisher*, or even 'Duke' class No. 3283 *Comet* or perhaps even 'Dukedogs' No. 3215 or 3223 were rostered to them. Drivers sometimes found that all their skill was required to control trains on the sharply falling gradients, and that the co-operation of their firemen was always essential. I experienced this sort of thing myself with No. 3283 *Comet*.

I had a ballast train for unloading at Newbury East Junction and the difficulty was not in getting up the banks, but in running off the branch into Newbury where the line crossed the West of England main line. Although my fireman had started to use the handbrake well back, soon after passing Hermitage, to check the wagons behind us, there did not seem to be any appreciable slackening in the speed of our train! It was raining heavily, and I had already used a considerable amount of sand to keep the wheels from slipping when climbing the banks. Over Fisher's Lane Crossing I decided to apply the vacuum-brake. Immediately the wheels locked, and the weight of the train pushing caused the engine to simply slide along the rails. I used the sanding apparatus to counteract this and, thankfully, the wheels began to grip once more, although our speed was still excessive. Next I used the brake whistle, to instruct the guard to apply more pressure on his handbrake. All I could do now was to carefully apply a small but increasing amount of vacuum. Still running too fast, we passed over London Road Bridge at Newbury, but then our brakes gradually took effect and we finally came to a stand. As I breathed a sigh of relief, a voice on the ground was heard to say 'Set back a little, driver, we want to unload further back!'

I retain some affection for the old *Comet*, perhaps because of incidents like this. On another occasion, during the period when the Didcot to Newbury line was being doubled, we had been at work at Fisher's Lane Crossing, and had made up a train of 35 or so empty ballast wagons. We began the long haul back to Didcot but, upon approaching Hermitage, my fireman informed me that the exhaust injector had stopped working. I decided not to stop and examine the injector myself as I was quite satisfied that my fireman had already done all that could be done, and that we could carry on by using the other injector. All locomotives were fitted with two injectors, with the exhaust injector being used whilst running and the other when standing. Since it should only be on very rare occasions that both injectors should be in use at the same time, I was not unduly worried about the situation.

As usual, we passed through Hampstead Norris at a considerable speed, in order to keep the loose-coupled wagons tight on the various dips and rises in the gradient. It was then I noticed that my fireman was peering over the side of the cab. It was now very dark, and he was trying to ascertain if the injector was working. It was not; steam and water were blowing back from the boiler into the waste water pipe. I glanced at the boiler water level gauge glass and, for the moment, we had, despite our all out dash through Hampstead Norris, a full boiler of water.

At Compton, I stopped the train at the station platform, and told my fireman to go to the signal box and tell the signalman that we were a failure, but that we would try to remedy the situation. In fact, this was now quite desperate. We had a roaring fire in the firebox and steam escaping from the safety-valves, a situation which could very easily use all the water in the boiler, but we were unable to put any more water in because of the failure of both injectors.

Apparently the injectors had got hot and, as sometimes happened, the clack box had failed to shut, so I poured buckets of cold water from the tender over the injector clack boxes, (another method was to tap the clack box, to get the ball valve to drop into position). I had no success, and even with my fireman's assistance was unable to get either injector to work. I then rang the Running Foreman at Didcot Shed from the signal box, and told him what had happened. He did not seem very concerned because all he said was, 'Whatever you do Alf, don't drop them plugs!', which really meant that I could make my own decision, provided that I prevented any damage to the fusible plugs in the firebox. What he really meant was 'put the fire out'. Fusible plugs were incorporated in all steam locomotives, their purpose being to prevent serious damage to the boiler should it become empty of water whilst the engine had a fire in the firebox. These plugs were made of lead so the temperature of the fire, with no water in the boiler, would melt them, hence the term used by enginemen 'dropping the plugs', which prevented serious damage being done.

Upon returning to the engine, I found that my fireman had been unable to start either injector so I said to him, 'Get the long fire-dropping shovel down, Jack; we'll have to throw the fire out'. We both took it in turns to do this. I was watching the water level in the boiler gauge glass all the time, but we were fighting a losing battle — we had only half a boiler of water, but the quantity of red hot clinker in the firebox was stopping us throwing out sufficient fire to stop the engine making steam. With a long chisel bar I was able to punch a hole in the fire. This relieved the situation a great deal, but the engine was still simmering at the safety-valves, and every bit of steam which escaped reduced the water level in the boiler. There was also a much larger loss from the injector clack boxes. I decided, therefore, that we would have to put the fire out by ballasting it with anything available, in this case the wet earth by the station platform fence. Backwards and forwards we went with bucketful and shovelful of whatever seemed suitable in the dark, to throw into the firebox. Keeping an eye on the boiler water gauge glass told me that there was only about an inch of water showing in the glass. Gradually the steam pressure dropped, but we were still losing water from the boiler too quickly. Then, from 160lb., the pressure began to drop rapidly down to 50lb. — the fire was out, and we had saved the firebox. It had been a gigantic struggle against time but we had made it, although the floor of the firebox was covered with dirt and ballast.

Eventually, another engine arrived from Didcot, to pull us and our train into Didcot Yard. The next day, when passing through Compton in daylight, we noticed huge holes against the platform fence, and the lovely rose-bushes, which had formerly been planted there, were scattered around them. Somehow, I felt unable to enlighten the stationmaster as to how it had happened!

By the way, it may be that the name *Comet* was somehow appropriate in the circumstances!

Steadily, the remodelling of the Didcot — Newbury — Winchester line progressed towards its completion. Unfortunately, this meant that the twelve upgraded firemen would soon be back to firing again although, in fact, it was not to be very long before I passed for driving officially. Before moving on to that however, an encounter with an 'ROD' as a fireman would not be out of place.

Although I had gained much experience as a fireman on these engines, it was always without any great success. It could be that I was used to working on locomotives with higher boiler pressure, and that when tackling the 'ROD's' 165lb. steam pressure, I never seemed able to maintain this, against what the driver was using, with the simultaneous use of the injectors. It could not be argued that they were necessarily old, since the first had been built for the Great Central Railway a good ten years after the first of our 2800 class had been completed. It is true that those which we had on the GWR had been built for the War Office during World War I, and had probably had a good deal of mistreatment. Anyway, it always seemed to me that the bad coal which these engines frequently had loaded into their tenders as well as the heavy loads put behind them, always combined to ensure a rough trip. One drawback was the provision of a steam brake only, and obviously, since this depended for its effectiveness on the boiler pressure, an 'ROD' performing badly could be expected to have equally poor braking power.

Suffice it to mention an experience with No. 3017, from the latter end of 1943. Fred Essex was my driver, and we had a freight train from Didcot to Westbury for working via Compton and Newbury. We were fully loaded with a train of power-station slack, and such a load over this route was a stiff job with a good engine, let alone a bad one.

We managed to keep going until we reached Upton Station, but at this point, Fred decided to allow me a few minutes to get a full head of steam and plenty of water in the boiler before facing the long upward climb through the cutting to East Ilsley. After leaving Upton, we steadily plodded our way up the rising gradient, but we were losing steam, and then the water dropped dangerously. After working flat out, I regained maximum pressure, but immediately lost it in raising the water level. Fred had the regulator three-quarters open, with 45 per cent cut off, and the surrounding country-side was being blasted with sparks and ashes from the chimney. This heavy handling was unavoidable for we had to keep going as there were two sets of spring catch points before reaching the top of the bank, and had we come to a stand astride them, we should have been unable to restart, even with a full head of steam.

I have never worked on an engine pulling a train at such a slow crawl without actually stalling. The engine seemed to be screaming that it could go no further, steam pressure was down to 100lb., and the injectors were on simply to keep water in the boiler. I was drenched in sweat, and we were both very dirty. At last we topped the bank, and Fred began to smile — all would be well on the other climbs. At Savernake, there was a stiffish climb again, but if I could maintain steam and water at maximum until we reached this point, we hoped that it would be taken in our stride. Passing Bedwyn, we began to approach Savernake and easing the regulator slightly, Fred took in the situation at a glance and then we were all out, thundering through Savernake Station at just over 30m.p.h. The side rods were clanking in protest at every revolution of the wheels and, for a short time, I began to think the steam gauge had become a fixture, so long did it remain at 160lb. Then, as it dropped to 150lb., the long haul started again — sweat, coal dust, hot cinders and ashes; the air around seemed full of it. I noticed how the speed had started to decrease, but I was cheered almost immediately as we passed through Savernake Station.

Fred then shut the regulator, sat down thankfully, got out his pipe and tobacco and lit up. He said, 'All downhill now, Alf, to Westbury.' I saw him do this many times at this point, but this was undoubtedly the most memorable.

RAILWAYS BETWEEN DIDCOT AND BIRMINGHAM

NOTE: Not all stations are shown, particularly in the Birmingham area.

Key

Great Western lines
LMS lines

LNER(GCR) lines.
x Honeybourne(Campden) Tunnel

to WOLVERHAMPTON

B'HAM SNOW HILL
TYSELEY
EARLSWOOD LAKES
HATTON
to B'HAM NEW STREET
LEAMINGTON SPA
STRATFORD ON-AVON
FENNY COMPTON
WOODFORD
to WORCESTER
HONEYBOURNE
GW BANBURY
to CHELTENHAM GLOUCESTER and BRISTOL
KINGHAM
to PADDINGTON
WITNEY
OXFORD
FAIRFORD
to DIDCOT

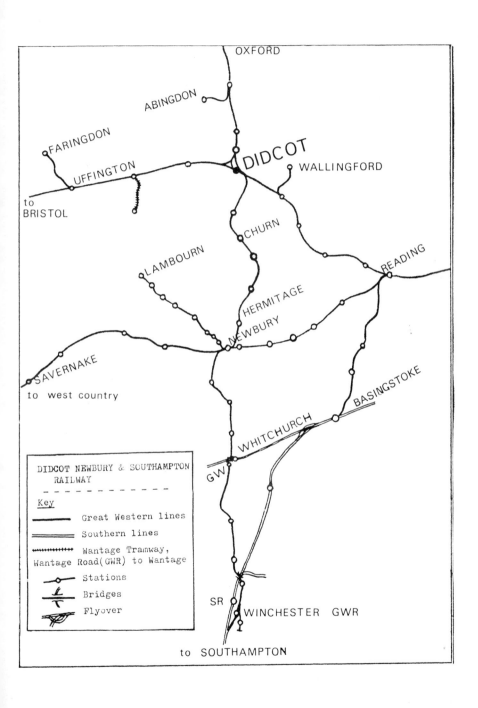

OXFORD

ABINGDON

FARINGDON

UFFINGTON

DIDCOT

WALLINGFORD

to
BRISTOL

CHURN

LAMBOURN

HERMITAGE

READING

NEWBURY

SAVERNAKE

to west country

BASINGSTOKE

WHITCHURCH

GW

DIDCOT NEWBURY & SOUTHAMPTON
RAILWAY
– – – – – – – – –
Key

———————— Great Western lines

═══════════ Southern lines

┼┼┼┼┼┼┼┼┼┼┼┼ Wantage Tramway,
Wantage Road(GWR) to Wantage

Stations

Bridges

Flyover

SR

WINCHESTER   GWR

to SOUTHAMPTON

Now in retirement, the author poses beside the replica GWR Royal Train at the Madame Tussauds exhibition at Windsor (Central) Station.

L. A. Summers

Above: 'Dukedog' 4-4-0, No. 3283 *Comet*, on a freight working at Reading West Junction in September 1943.   *M. W. Earley*

Below: Although a modern photograph of a preserved locomotive, this picture of No. 3217 (No. 9017) *Earl of Berkeley*, is typical of the GWR scene on the secondary lines where 4-4-0s predominated.
L. A. Summers

Although the author never drove 9F 2-10-0 *Evening Star*, he often had other members of the class.

L. A. Summers

Above: The original 'King', No. 6000 *King George V* makes a splendid sight as it passes through the streets of Bath with a special train in 1971.

L. A. Summers

Below: The spirit of the GWR in the 20th century is summed up by this view of a Great Western railtour in 1974, double-headed by No. 7808 *Cookham Manor* and No. 6998 *Burton Agnes Hall*.

L. A. Summers

2-8-0 tank No. 5239 crosses Churston Viaduct on the Paignton to Kingswear section of the Dart Valley Railway.

L. A. Summers

King George V at the Great Western Society's Didcot centre on 26th June 1983.

L. A. Summers

2-8-0 tank, No. 5239, at Kingswear in the hot summer of 1983, some
46 years after the author's first visit.

L. A. Summers

Above: Locomotive charade! Although carrying the name and numberplates of No. 4082 *Windsor Castle*, this is in fact No. 7013 *Bristol Castle*! It is pictured on pilot duties at Paddington, in Spring 1964, shortly before withdrawal.   *L. A. Summers*

Below: A 5101 class 2-6-2 tank, No. 5164, built in 1930. These engines differed little from the 61XX series and worked the same type of trains.   *L. A. Summers*

Above: Pannier tank No. 3751. These engines were the GWR 'Maid of all work' types.

L. A. Summers

Below: A typical Didcot cross wind blows the smoke from a 'Modified Hall', on an 'up' fast freight, across the front of the cab. The photograph was taken towards the close of Western Region steam operation.

L. A. Summers

Above: Standard GWR 2-6-2 tank, No. 6136, at Oxford.

L. A. Summers

Below: An almost timeless Western steam scene. 'Castle' class, No. 5054 *Earl of Ducie*, simmers at Paddington after its arrival from Worcester.

L. A. Summers

Above: The Wantage Tramway 0-4-0WT *Jane* (seen at work by the author on many occasions) stands in retirement at Didcot, and forms a striking contrast with Liverpool & Manchester Railway 0-4-0 *Lion*.

B. J. Summers

Below: A very famous locomotive — 'Castle' class 4-6-0, No. 4079 *Pendennis Castle*. The author cleaned, fired and drove this locomotive during his long career.

L. A. Summers

CHAPTER FIVE

I was now high up in my position as one of the senior firemen at Didcot, and decided to join the Mutual Improvement Class. I knew that the examination for driver involved quite a considerable amount of railway knowledge such as signalling rules, technical details and so on. The Mutual Improvement Class was actually conducted by the men themselves, with the Company's encouragement of course, and drivers like Jack Wigley, George Barnes and Harry Walker, who were wholly reliable to teach the facts about locomotive preparation and running, conducted these classes.

Despite the continued success of the allied forces, the railway companies were still finding it necessary to promote more firemen to driver. However, the trend was entirely different from that of the early years of the war, when men had been promoted to replace those killed in bombing raids. Now, more and more troop movements were being made by rail, and more and more trains conveying tanks and munitions were being run. When working the 7.38 Didcot to Southampton passenger train with Bill Darby, we could see for ourselves, along the roads adjoining the railway, stretching towards Winchester and Southampton, the daily sight of military vehicles driven almost bumper to bumper in ever increasing numbers. It was obvious that something big was building up, because this traffic reached a point where the railways were unable to handle any more.

Hence my decision to join the Mutual Improvement Class. I knew that there was still a lot I had to learn about train running, while I especially had to know the rules relative to footplate work. There could be no errors, as no margin would be allowed for failure. My thoughts went back to Charlie Brown, who had said that I would know 'more than nothing' when I left him. It was good training, and I had reason to be grateful for that early encouragement.

Reality, in the form of a paper instructing me to report to Swindon for the purpose of 'examination by the Inspector for promotion', awaited me when I booked on for duty in May 1944. I had less than one week in which to complete my knowledge although, at this stage, I did feel quite confident. A neighbour, also a driver, came in the night before to ask me the kind of questions that would be put at Swindon and, after two hours of this, pronounced himself satisfied. He said that I had nothing to fear, which gave me added confidence. The actual examination at Park House took 35 minutes, and I remember that, at one point, the Inspector enquired if I had been born in

Berkshire because I spoke like a Londoner. When I told him that, previous to coming to Didcot, I had been at Old Oak Common, he smiled and said, 'Well then, you can answer me some questions about the four cylinder classes, having seen and worked on them.' This I did and, after congratulating me on the clearness and promptness of my answers, he shook my hand saying, 'You have passed as a driver.' I was now an engine driver and I had passed my examination on 5th June 1944, a much more unforgettable date to me than the rather more important event which took place early the following morning.

Of course, to take charge of a locomotive was no new experience to me. In fact, I had previously worked about 300 jobs whilst still a fireman, but the feeling now was different; I had put down the fireman's shovel, and had taken on a vastly more responsible role. Looking at it another way, I had now reached, as it is said, every boy's ambition. Upon reflection, however, I wonder if the little boy could remain as enthusiastic, realising that it was not always the glamorous job he might think. The drivers of today's enthusiast steam trains like the 'Cumbrian Mountain Express' cannot really relive the real steam railway unless, of course, they were, themselves, drivers and firemen of steam engines in the days before 1968.

Imagine a nice warm bed, on a cold and frosty night. It is 3a.m. when your alarm clock suddenly shrieks out, telling you that it is time to get up, and as you sleepily open your eyes to stop this awful din, it seems to be laughing with maniacal frenzy. You lay there, looking at the face of the clock, but still it ticks loudly away. As the seconds grind on, you make the attempt to get out of bed; it leers at you, knowing that you have got to obey its irreversible message. You then come down the stairs into the kitchen, dress, make a cup of tea, collect your sandwiches made by your wife (who is still tucked up in bed) and look out of the window. The ground is white — has it been snowing? You put on your overcoat over a spotless set of overalls, made by Compton, Son & Webb at Swindon, and your driver's cap. You eventually leave your home, and immediately slip on the icy pavement. After recovering your balance, you huddle into your overcoat and plod down the road to the locomotive shed, where you bawl out to the time clerk, 'Book me on, Mark', whereupon he gives you your special speed notices, and you look at the duty roster. You already know your turn of duty, but you have to ascertain what locomotive you have been allocated.

Your heart sinks! The engine is No. 2822, offering no protection from the elements while preparing it for the job, and only a short cab when running. Still, at least it is a reliable engine, and that's something. You then walk round to where it is situated, on the pits outside the shed. The icy wind catches you as you hang up your overcoat, and don your oiling overalls which you have collected from your locker. Your fireman has not yet arrived so you go back to the stores to get the tool box keys. You then open the tool box, only to find that the oil cans are frozen to the bottom of the box. Eventually you dislodge them, take them to the stores and are given a quantity of oil, paraffin and cotton waste. Your fireman arrives, and grunts out a 'Good morning, Alf'. He is not in a much better mood than you!

You next fill your feeder with oil; although it was warm when collected from the stores, it has now got cold and will hardly run. You go down into the pit underneath the engine, and are at once thankful that it has only two cylinders. You then try to pull yourself up by the eccentric rods but there is ice all over them. Your hand slips, so you grab the back gear eccentric to hoist yourself up. Now, with hands almost numb with the cold, you try to remove the eccentric corks. They won't move, so you stand and fume. All the time the wind whistles to you as it comes in under the boiler. After trying again, you succeed in removing three of the corks, and you fill the oil wells. The fourth is stubborn. It breaks off, so you get out your pocket corkscrew, hold it in your numb hand and manage to pull out the remains of the cork. You have not got a fresh one in your pocket, so you shout for the fireman to bring you one. He cannot hear because he has put on the injector, and hot water runs down from the clack box delivery pipe which is apparently leaking. The water runs all over you while standing under the locomotive so you give up, and come out from under the engine to have a look at it. Next you inform the mechanical staff about the fault, bring some corks from the stores and go into the pit again to continue your oiling. After completing the work underneath, you come out, and start to oil the connecting rods. Your teeth begin to chatter because it is getting to be really cold, while your fireman is sweating on the footplate; this makes you feel even colder. You climb up on to the footplate to try to warm your hands, but your fireman is on the back of the tender, throwing huge lumps of coal forward to make up a good fire. So you quickly get down again and pick up your oil feeder to carry on oiling, but now the oil is really cold and will hardly run at all. You have, therefore, to warm it up with steam from the injector waste water pipe.

The fitters have stopped the leak from the clack box joint and your fireman is ready, so you wash your hands and remove your dirty overalls, putting them in the lockers. Upon returning to the engine, you find that the fireman has made a can of tea. After noting that all is clear you open the regulator and move the engine down towards the shed outlet signal, where the fireman phones the signalman and tells him where you are to pick up your train. The fireman then returns to tell you that the signalman says that the shed to main line points are frozen, and that we are to go back to the shed to await orders! It is now 5a.m., and snowing heavily . . . so you want to be an engine driver!

In the last year or so of the war, when the minimum delay to trains was essential, it was thought more expedient to let the locomotives work through to the train's destination, rather than to prepare a fresh engine to work the train on when it had reached a company boundary. In these circumstances I found myself taking over from LMS men on 'Black Five' locomotives or from LNER men on the 'Austerity' type. It seemed that we encountered most types of freight locomotive, whether it was of LMS, LNER or Southern origin. Then, perhaps, we would have our own engines for a couple of days, and then relieve Southern men on an old SECR 4-4-0 or perhaps even a 'Merchant Navy' Pacific. The latter, unlike the GWR engines, had electric lights in the cab, but I always switched them off when taking over one of these engines.

The locomotive shortage was acute, and for working stopping goods trains between Didcot and Reading, or Didcot and Swindon, we were given old Midland Johnson 0-6-0 tender engines. These locomotives were a nightmare to GWR men. No doubt, in their day, they had done some good work on the Midland, but to us they were always a source of unreliability and uncertainty. I remember one particular time, after leaving Didcot with just nine loaded wagons for Swindon, we had just proceeded down the main line towards Lockinge when the steam pressure and the water level began to fall alarmingly. Apparently, my fireman had the impression that the injectors were putting water into the boiler, but with the drop in steam pressure I at once realised that this was not so. Instead, the water was escaping via the waste pipe, due to an overheated clack box on the delivery pipe.

I immediately stopped the train, as it was clearly impossible to go any further in this condition. I sent my fireman on foot to Lockinge West signal box, to inform the signalman of our plight, and while he was gone I managed to get the injectors working again. As soon as he returned he began to shovel coal on the fire, and with a now healthy steam level we proceeded to Wantage Road Station, where we were turned off the main line into the sidings. A minute later, the 8.55 Paddington to Swansea train roared by, its 'Castle' belching black smoke as if it had been momentarily checked. We used to think that the Wantage Tramway engine *Jane* was an 'old un', but when I saw it pulling loaded coal wagons, I felt sure that it was fully equal to these dreadful Johnson engines. When I see that some of them were still at work in the late 1950s, I find myself speechless with amazement.

Such things as faulty injectors, bad coal, sluggish steaming and inexperienced firemen all helped to convince us that the driver was certainly the captain of the ship because, out on the main line, his were the decisions and no help could be given. Somehow we always seemed to get to our destination and, next day, would book on duty ready to have another go with the same class of engine. We worked on many classes of engine during this period, but it would be fair to say that there was a time when every engine, however old, had to be pressed into service. Although maintenance was not neglected, it was not, in these circumstances, first class. Superheaters would blow, injectors would be faulty, tubes would be blocked, bad coal would be on the tender, and fires would not be properly cleaned; but these were items which could not stop a locomotive from operating, and when trains with important freight for the successful continuation of the Second Front in Europe were standing in the yards waiting for power, defective engines had to be rushed into service. The locomotive men knew their faults, but refusal to work a train with such an engine was akin to sabotage, although against our principles. Sometimes we would get excellent engines for weeks, and that was lucky, while the less fortunate got the bad ones more often. Some firemen could get steam from coal dust and dirt, but others were always, it seemed, struggling to maintain steam pressure, with all the odds against succeeding.

Where I was, in the junior driving links, there were many firemen who were just learning how to manage a big engine. The inexperience of some of these young men was most marked as, unfortunately, some had been promoted from cleaner to fireman, and had been sent to Didcot after having graduated from some small shed in South Wales, where they had not even seen a tender engine before. In these circumstances, the driver would, whenever possible, try to instruct his mate on how to form the fire efficiently. On several occasions while stopped for signals, I have done this, building up the fire with the shovel until we have regained a full head of steam. My fireman was, I always hoped, watching closely, and learning something from my activity.

For a long time we had American servicemen in this country, but now we were using their locomotives on our railways. After an

61

initial briefing about the various differences in the driving technique, we found that, with a heavy freight train, their performance was quite good. Despite this, however, there was no parallel with a GWR engine, and it would have to have been very good indeed for GWR men to say differently. I have found that this was also so of other men. While GWR men never really felt happy in charge of an 'Austerity' 2-8-0, the LNER drivers were full of praise for them. To us, the Class 8F 2-8-0s, built by Stanier for the LMS, were never in the same league as the GWR 'Hall' class, despite the closeness of their design.

Another engine which had long ago seen its best days was No. 1335. This was one of three Midland & South Western Junction Railway 2-4-0s, built in 1894 and later rebuilt with a GWR boiler. These locomotives were intended for express passenger work, or such as the MSWJR ran, but were retained by the GWR long after its own 2-4-0s had been cut up, as they were very suitable for short branch line work. Nos. 1334 and 1336 were kept at Reading, but No. 1335 was stabled at Didcot to work horse-box specials and passenger trains on the Lambourn Valley line, and from Didcot to Newbury. We would leave Didcot with three coaches on a Sunday afternoon, and stop at all stations enroute to Lambourn.

The driving and firing positions in the cab were very cramped but it always gave a comfortable ride and although the engine had to be nursed for much of the way, we were never really in trouble. It was a thing of wonderment to me that such an engine worked passenger trains but this, of course, was because the District Engineer could not sanction anything heavier on the Lambourn branch. Fortunately, on arrival at Newbury, sufficient time was allowed for us to take the engine to Newbury Racecourse Yard turntable, where we could turn the engine so that when we left Newbury for Lambourn, we were proceeding tender first. This allowed us to return to Newbury and Didcot head first, as there were no turning facilities at Lambourn.

By early 1945, it was obvious that Germany was going to be defeated. In April 1945, the Luftwaffe had been sufficiently eclipsed for black-out restrictions to be lifted, which came as a tremendous relief to engine crews. Then, in May, the end of the war in Europe came, but it was going to be a long time before the railways were able to get back to normal peace-time working. Much of the coaching stock was in need of repair, many of the freight wagons which had been kept in use were now ready for the scrap yard, whilst some locomotives, which had been worked without proper maintenance, were beyond profitable repair.

Perhaps the most far reaching aftermath of the war was the 1945 General Election and the return of Mr Attlee's Labour Government, the first with a clear working majority. Committed to a programme of social reform and public ownership, Labour nationalised the railways from 1st January 1948, so bringing to an end 110 years of Great Western Railway history. On that cold January day, an era came to an end. No more, or so we thought, would we see the GWR insignia emblazoned on locomotives and rolling stock. As it turned out, outward evidence of the GWR took a long time to die, as in 1957, *Tregenna Castle* was still running paired with a tender which carried the austerity version of the GWR coat of arms, while some of the tank engines on Paddington empty stock workings were still in the 1930s GWR livery styles, staying this way almost until the end of 1958.

Nationalisation meant little immediate change to the mass of 'working' railwaymen, but to their new owners, the vastness of the problem which had been set before them soon began to show. I would describe the situation as being rather similar to that of a child who has played with his train set for a number of years and then, suddenly, is forced to the conclusion that if he wants to use it for very much longer, practically everything would have to be renewed. The new owners of the railways were forced to embark upon a huge programme of modern replacements and, in some respects, this has been ongoing ever since. For the time being, however, the old railway companies' Chief Mechanical Engineers were allowed certain freedom of action, and the locomotive programme of the GWR continued almost unaltered for some years. Although, subsequently, the post-war locomotive policy of the Great Western Railway has been seriously criticised, the maintenance of well-tried and competent designs had its attractions.

Most of the locomotive types of the GWR have come within my sphere of duties, and I have often been asked to venture an opinion as to what were the best. This is not easy to answer, but I think that I would settle for the 2800 class 2-8-0 freight locomotive. The first of these were built as long ago a 1903 and the last only in 1942 and, in my view, they were never superseded; their pulling power was amazing. I have arrived in marshalling yards with this class of engine and, when seeing the length and weight of the train, have thought, 'She'll never pull it!' Upon leaving the yard, (Banbury would be a fair example, where every locomotive was loaded to its full capacity), and pulling out on to the main line, the speed would gradually increase and the exhaust from the 2800's chimney would resound each time like the bark from a demented animal. Despite this, the power of this engine overcame all difficulty. Whether the train went up severe inclines or wherever, it was just the same in performance; a little less speed might be observed, but the engine would pull and continue to do so. Never in all my considerble experience of driving did I find the equal to the 2800 class among the other companies' locomotives. It is a curious fact that when seeing a 2800 class standing next to a 'Castle', visitors to locomotive sheds would spare little time to look at the freight engine. The 'Castle', magnificent in its splended livery, would over-shadow the 2800, but never could the 'Castle' dim the efficient record of these engines.

Little is known about the 5ft. 8in. 4700 class 2-8-0s, but these, in my opinion, were another excellent engine, a long way ahead of other companies' mixed traffic types. Although they had been built for mixed traffic workings in the first place, they also performed very well on fast fully-fitted perishable freight trains. These usually ran at night, so the 4700s were rarely seen in action during daylight, which may account for their relative obscurity. As a fireman at Old Oak Common, I had many trips on these engines, and was convinced that they were excellent engines; the large boiler and high steam pressure always indicating the makings of a good trip for both driver and fireman. They were not booked to run at express train speed, but once out on the road they were able to maintain a high speed, and we were rarely behind schedule due to a fault with the locomotive, hence their use on passenger trains and, in some cases, on expresses during the height of the summer season. Of course, like all really big-boilered engines, it was a little difficult to see along the side of the boiler, from inside the cab, when observing the signals on circuitous routes. The assistance of the fireman, however, easily overcame this difficulty. The two cylinder 2-8-0s almost always conveyed a full load, formed of box wagons sometimes containing soap from Port Sunlight or sugar from the Tate & Lyle refineries at Liverpool. Wolverhampton-based 4700s would be in charge of these trains. Only nine of the class were built, and apart from Wolverhampton only Old Oak Common and Plymouth (Laira) ever had an allocation.

Didcot men would get a 4700 class engine on the 3.25a.m. Acton Yard to Bristol (Kingsland Road) service, working it from their home depot. This was loaded with up to 58 box vans; a heavy train, but well within the capabilities of the locomotive if the fireman was efficient. It would be pitch dark as we walked from the shed to Didcot Station and invariably, within a couple of minutes of our arrival there, the train would run in. We would pause only to exchange particulars with the Southall men about the engine and load, and would soon be on our way. The very gradual uphill rise all the way to Swindon would tell me the condition of the engine. Sometimes, it would just be getting light as we passed Uffington, with the famous white horse mistily visible in the far distance.

At Swindon Goods Yard, we would draw in to detach wagons and then be on our way again, passing the vast panorama of Swindon Works as we gathered speed to run to Chippenham, where we would call for the same purpose. After leaving Chippenham, we would soon be approaching Box Tunnel, and after coming out of the tunnel we would go round the winding curves in the track with, on the right, lorries making their way to Bath, laden with market produce. Travelling the road as only early risers can, virtually with it all to themselves, they were able to make a fair pace, but a road lorry could never beat a train, either for speed or sheer pulling power.

At Kingsland Road Yard, the shunter would release the engine, regaling us with some remark such as 'Have you come across the fields?', if we were early. We would take the engine to St. Philip's Marsh Shed, which housed shunting and freight engines, where it would be left, after which we would go for a wash because the run was a hard one, and left us pretty grubby.

Another type of GWR engine which tends to be forgotten these days is the 7200 class 2-8-2T, these being powerful engines that were used mainly on heavy South Wales coal trains. Their main drawback was that when leaving those areas, they did not carry enough water for long stretches where water-columns were not available. Even these big tanks suffered from the drawback of all tank engines, in that the cab, unlike that of a tender engine, was very confined. However, they did have more shelter for the enginemen, and in bad weather allowed the coal to be always accessible to the fireman. On tender engines, after the coal had been used from the front of the tender, the fireman had to go into the tender, sometimes at very high speed and in very bad weather, to pull more forward from the back. As a passenger fireman I always endeavoured to get as much coal forward as possible before leaving the shed but, on long runs, it was always impossible to get sufficient forward. Sometimes we would even return to the shed with just coal dust left in the tender. Fortunately, there were washing facilities in the enginemen's cabins, and we were able to wash before leaving for home.

One type of engine to which I was introduced at a relatively late stage was the 0-4-2 branch line tank, my first meeting with them taking place on the Wallingford branch. This branch ran from Wallingford to the main line station at Cholsey, a distance of 2¾ miles. Although the branch was under Didcot's control, the locomotive was maintained at Wallingford by a resident shedman and was housed in a miniature shed opposite the single face platform. Two sets of locomotive men, who lived at Wallingford, maintained the passenger service between them, there being no trains after about 10p.m. and before 6.55a.m. Therefore, by working their eight hour shifts of early turn one week and afternoons alternately, the train service was covered adequately. For many years, the drivers on this line were two brothers by the name of Frewin and, purely unofficially of course, they shared out the roster to suit their own domestic arrangements. I have no doubt that officialdom knew what was going on, but as there were never any mishaps, they closed their eyes to it.

When one of the regular men was ill or on annual leave, a driver was sent to Wallingford to fill in for him. Eventually one of them retired, and it was decided that all men in the passenger link at Didcot should know the 'road', and familiarise themselves with the procedures on this branch. At one point, the driver from Didcot was taken to and from Wallingford by contract taxi, a most uneconomic arrangement, but later the sensible course of keeping the engine at Didcot, and working the line from there was adopted.

I well remember my first turn of duty on the Wallingford branch, after learning the road, which ran from Cholsey to Wallingford through unspoiled rural countryside. Booking on at Didcot Shed, early on the Tuesday morning, I was conveyed to Wallingford by taxi from outside Didcot Station. At Wallingford my fireman, a local man, had already obtained the shed key, and was busy getting up steam for our first trip. For me, this was, in fact, my first turn on a 1400 class 0-4-2T.

These engines may have looked rather old as, indeed, they were, being based on an Armstrong design dating back to 1873, but were in fact, modernised versions, as it had been found that this type of engine was the most successful on the type of work envisaged. Other railways did not build such 'old looking' tanks so late in the day, simply because they had far more really old tanks in the 1930s than the GWR ever had. Another, and perhaps surprising bonus was that they were good little 'goers', with one being recorded at 67m.p.h. on a one coach train in the late 1950s. Nos. 1407, 1409, 1444 and 1447 were the regular performers on the branch at one time and I seem to recall that No. 1442, the locomotive preserved at Tiverton, was also used on the branch.

After preparing the engine, we then ran round on to the auto-coach which formed our train for the day and, after having coupled up the auto-car and the driving connections for the car's driving cab, we shunted into the platform. That first train had about fourteen passengers, and we sped along the single line like a greyhound. There was no doubt that these little engines could move themselves, which was just as well, as although it was not very far to Cholsey, we were not allowed a great deal of time, usually only about six minutes. Any late start from Wallingford would mean that the main line trains to and from Paddington, which stopped at Cholsey, would be delayed. At Cholsey, I would leave the engine and go to the driving end of the auto-car, where regulator, vacuum-brake and handbrake connections to the engine, and rail sanding equipment were provided. The handbrake, rather than the vacuum-brake, was used for stopping the trains on the line. There were no signals on the branch, except at the terminus where they were operated by the porter/signalman/shunter. Also, at the Cholsey end, there were signals operated from the main line box. We would complete seven trips from Wallingford and seven the other way during this turn of duty, and then return to Didcot Shed to book off.

The railways attracted a lot of popular attention in the 1950s, as a result of a number of serious accidents. I was never actually involved in anything that might be described as 'serious', although of my three mishaps, one was potentially very serious indeed. I will come to that later, but the first incident, from my very early days at Didcot, occurred whilst my turn of duty included marshalling the engines in their departure procedure in the shed. I was moving a tender engine from one road to another, when I collided with a 2900 'Saint' class locomotive which had crossed my path. The 'Saint', manned by Leamington men, was on its way to the turntable and unfortunately, by catching its tender sideways, the buffers of my engine pushed it off the road. I screwed the engine down and had a few 'words' with the other driver. He had been in the wrong for not seeing, before running foul, that engine movements were being made in the shed.

The Running Foreman was, naturally, most annoyed, but to the mechanical staff the re-railing of the tender was a simple matter. My engine had to be taken out of service, however, because the buffer beam had been damaged. Mishaps like this were not uncommon and one Didcot driver, notable in local politics, had something of a reputation for knocking down the shed doors!

Another incident, although of a rather different kind, occurred when I was learning the road and was travelling back from Washwood Heath Sidings on the footplate of a 'Hall', which was hauling a freight train for Southampton Docks. When approaching St. Andrew's Junction, passing along the back of Birmingham City's football ground, just before we passed under a bridge, I was observing the signals whilst standing close up in the corner and looking through the fireman's spectacle glass. Suddenly the window was shattered by a stone, apparently dropped by children on the bridge who, it seemed, were trying to drop it down the chimney of the engine. After missing the chimney, the stone had bounced along the boiler and hit the window.

My first impulse was to brush the fragments of glass from my face, but a timely shout from the fireman made me hesitate. 'Don't touch your face or open your eyes' he said, 'your face is covered with glass splinters'. The driver, after seeing that the situation was serious, stopped the train at Bordesley Junction, where he reported to the signalman what had happened. Meanwhile, the fireman used his handkerchief to gently brush the fragments of glass from my face. All this time I had clung to the side of the cab with my eyes tightly shut and now, I was almost afraid to open them. To my intense relief they were not damaged, but I decided to get off the engine to pick the fragments out of my clothes and wash my face. I thanked the driver and fireman for their great assistance and got down.

The majority of younger train-spotters are well-behaved, but there are those who will not confine themselves to a safe position on the platforms, and will sit with their legs hanging dangerously near to oncoming express trains. In consequence they were, at one time, banned completely at some places. Irresponsible children, and indeed very stupid adults as well, have been responsible for many accidents on the railway. I mention the adults in particular, because my son tells me that whenever special steam trains run, there is always a minority of so-called railway enthusiasts who persist in going into highly dangerous places to get photographs.

Anyway, I phoned the police from the ground signalman's cabin, more as a matter of form rather than with any belief that it would be of much use as before they could get to the bridge, the culprits would be gone. When I removed my clothes, I found blood on my shirt collar and tie. I made my way back to Didcot Shed and reported the incident to the Running Foreman. Only then did I learn that my face was pitted in many places with cuts and bloody marks. I shall always remember that Tyseley fireman; there is no doubt that had I opened my eyes immediately, I should have been blinded for life, and his quick thinking saved my eyesight.

An incident of far more serious, or rather potentially serious, consequence to the travelling public occurred when I was working an excursion from Slough, with a 4-6-0 'Hall' No. 6983 *Otterington Hall.* We had taken the empty stock for the special from Didcot and brought it into the 'up' relief platform at Slough, so we then ran round the train to get to the departure end. We did not have to turn the engine, because we had left Didcot tender first to eliminate possible delay (the turntable at Slough Shed was not large enough to turn a 'Hall' so all turning of larger engines was done on Bath Road Triangle, a procedure which sometimes took a considerable time). After this was accomplished, and all passengers were aboard, we had the 'right away' from the guard and proceeded down the relief line to Reading East Main, where I was turned out on to the main line. The crossover from the relief line to the 'down' main was negotiated at reduced speed, there being a permanent speed restriction here which, in the circumstances, was indeed very fortunate.

Located at the London end of Reading Station, which I was now approaching, on the 'down' main line platform, was the GPO mail collecting and distribution area. Mails were collected in bags from various trains and placed in steel mesh-covered wagons, coupled together and hauled along the platform by a motorised unit to this centre. These motor units were painted red. As I approached the station, now increasing my speed as I was not stopping at Reading, although, nevertheless, booked to run through the platform road, I noticed a large red object lying in the track. At the same time the 'up' and 'down' main line platforms were packed with people awaiting trains, it being the height of the summer season, the majority probably were families going on holiday. Quickly I realised that this red object was a GPO motor van which had, apparently, been driven or had fallen off the edge of the platform and on to the tracks. As I bore down on it I noticed the figure of its driver trying to get clear, so my immediate reaction was to brake to stop clear of the obstruction. The train came to a halt about two yards from the motor unit.

As I brought my train to a stand, four GPO men and some of the station staff jumped down on to the track in front of my engine, and began the laborious task of manhandling the motor unit back on to the platform. In the meantime, I sent the fireman to telephone the signalman, and tell him why we had stopped. After about fifteen minutes, the track was cleared, and I proceeded on my way with the train. In the event, the incident was slight, but it could have had disastrous consequences. Had I been travelling at high speed, and had my attention been taken by something in the cab, the results could have been catastrophic. The engine and the first coaches of the train would have been thrown among the passengers waiting on platform 4 with terrifying consequences. Of course, I made a report about the matter, but it seemed to me that the authorities were more concerned with my having delayed the 'Cornish Riviera' than the possibility of a disastrous railway accident.

It was in the 1950s, as a result of the terrible double collision at Harrow, that automatic train control — what is now, perhaps more properly, called the automatic warning system — came under the public spotlight. It was much talked about at the time that the GWR had used a successful system of AWS since before World War I, while other railways had made little progress in this area. My experience was that automatic train control was a godsend, and one episode will serve to show this.

At one point, LNER drivers from Woodford Halse had a job through to Swindon, from which they returned light engine. During winter months, and particularly when it was foggy, they were inclined to hang about, partly because they could not see the signals clearly, and partly, it was suspected, in order to bump up their overtime. After a while, the GWR authorities got a little fed up with this, so they sent a GWR engine from Didcot to pilot them. We used to buffer up at the front end and couple the two engines together at Didcot West Curve, see that everything was all right, get the signal, and then go hell for leather through the fog, not stopping until we got to the north end of Oxford Station, where we were usually stopped. At this point the Woodford Halse driver would stagger up to our engine, shaking like a leaf and, with his face as black as thunder, promise, in no uncertain terms, to have all damnation brought down upon us!

Despite this, we were quite confident of what we had been doing. The comforting 'ting' of the ATC bell had been reassurance to us that all our signals had been at 'line clear', and that we were able to proceed safely. Of course, the automatic train control did not relieve us of the responsibility of observing the signals, but the Great Western Railway was usually years ahead of anyone else in its practices.

CHAPTER SIX

Didcot locomotive shed had very few main line express train duties, therefore, in the early 1940s, its tender engines were largely double-framed 4-4-0s, 'Dean Goods' locomotives and Moguls. However, it is not often remembered that Didcot had on its strength one of the 1500 class short wheelbase 0-6-0 pannier tanks, built by Hawksworth in 1949. This class of engine was almost unique as far as 20th century GWR locomotive practice was concerned. Apart from an isolated 0-4-0T built in 1902 and, of course the three 'De Glehn' Compounds, the GWR never produced an engine with the valve gear and motion attached to the driving wheels on the outside. Other companies had more or less standardised this arrangement in the 1920s, but the GWR had never fallen into line.

No. 1502 was allocated to Didcot for practically the whole of its working life. My experience of these engines, and they were in constant use, particularly on empty stock working at Paddington, was that their efficiency was beyond reproach. However, as far as enginemen were concerned, the ride on the footplate was rather like riding a rubber ball — there was too much 'bounce'. This, no doubt, was a result of the short wheelbase and the lack of leading and trailing wheels. One thing about these engines, that a GWR driver had never experienced before, but greatly appreciated, was that all parts which had to be lubricated in the course of preparing the engine to work, were accessible from ground level and this did away with the need to go inside.

The first 'Hall' to come to Didcot arrived in 1934. This was No. 5934 *Kneller Hall* named, I believe, after the Royal School of Military Music. There never was a very large staff of engine cleaners at Didcot but their engines had always been admired, and No. 5934 took pride of place. It was kept spotlessly clean, even to the point of oiling the boiler so that dirt and smuts were easier to clean off. Didcot enginemen, long used to the medium powered Moguls and 4-4-0s, when first faced with a 'Hall' were inclined to open the regulator too far upon starting, which caused the locomotive to slip madly. After the Newbury line had been doubled, in 1941, the stock of 'Hall' class engines gradually increased.

A great deal has already been written about the Newbury branch but, inevitably, it figures largely in my story. Its traffic was, after all, worked in the main by men from Didcot, and it was an important line even before it was doubled to Newbury during the war. You could, for instance, board the two LNER coaches attached to the 7.33 service from Southampton and finally alight far away in Newcastle, having stopped at every station to Didcot! Just imagine it, the luxury of a through train from the green hills of Upton and Blewbury to the soot black shores of the Tyne!

One of our turns of duty in the freight link at Didcot, around 1941, was the 4.30a.m. working to Winchester, running via Compton and Newbury. This train nearly always consisted of a full load, and was always double-headed by a 2251 class 0-6-0, with a 5700 class 0-6-0PT as the inside engine. On arrival at Newbury, the pannier tank became the Newbury Yard pilot and the traffic for that location, consisting mainly of coal for the gasworks, was detached. Newbury men would work the tank engine on pilot duties, while the Didcot men would take over yesterday's pilot engine at Newbury, and work three coaches back to Didcot as the 6.45a.m. passenger train. When they arrived back at Didcot, it was quite common to have used the last of the coal from the bunker, with the engine having just sufficient steam to run around the train, push it on to the stop blocks and then go off to the shed!

Booking on duty for this turn was at 3.30a.m., and we were allowed 45 minutes to prepare each of the engines for the train. A No. 2 link driver would be on the second engine whilst on the leading engine, the 2251 class, there would be a No. 3 link driver. Before leaving the shed the fireman would couple the engines together, and in the yard, we would back on to the train. Details of the load were always given by the guard to the driver on the leading engine, and passed to the second driver. The latter, by the way, was also required to observe all signals en route; this being stated in the rule book.

On getting 'line clear' on the signal, at the exit from the yard, which turned us on to the 'up' relief line, and also the green flag from the guard, we would proceed towards Didcot East Junction signal box, with the fireman on the second engine looking back to ascertain that the train was complete and following in the correct sequence. The fireman on the first engine would collect the Didcot to Compton single line staff when passing Didcot East Junction signal box. After this, both firemen would concentrate their attention on maintaining a full head of steam for the heavy pull to the top of Upton Bank near the village of East Ilsey.

Although already steep, when passing through Upton Station, the gradient would begin to rise even more and both engines would be working to capacity as, indeed, were the firemen. It was essential to keep going, as three spring catch points had to be passed. After arriving at the top of the bank, it would be downhill for a short way to Churn Halt — always known as the firemen's 'recovery time' — then uphill again to Compton. Here the first engine's fireman would change the 'staff' at the signal box for the one for the section to Hermitage. Running downhill from Compton and over Compton Crossing, the gradient now rose and fell until we were past Hampstead Norris. With this being a loose-coupled train consisting mainly of coal, it was imperative that the drivers went 'all out' to keep the couplings tight.

After passing Hampstead Norris there was a long pull uphill to Hermitage, passing Pinewood Halt on the way. At Hermitage Station, the single line 'staff' was changed for the one for the section to Newbury East Junction. Passing Fisher's Lane crossing, the gradient rose just enough to momentarily check the speed by applying the tender handbrake very gently. The fireman's experience of this was invaluable to his driver. Too much pressure and the train would come to a stand before reaching Newbury East Junction home signal, not enough pressure and the train, despite the driver gently applying the vacuum-brake, would pass the signal which was usually at 'stop'. Since there was a catch point just past the signal, the train would become derailed. This down gradient, from Hermitage to Newbury East, was such that the weight of a coal train could quickly get out of hand.

On both locomotives, steam was now shut off, with no power being needed as the weight of the train was pushing both engines at a speed which, if not reduced, would soon become uncontrollable. Drivers always had their trains under control, with the assistance of the guard using his handbrake in the van, but other elements such as a greasy rail or, as sometimes happened, leaves from lineside trees getting piled on to the rails in autumn or, perhaps, having used all the sand previously on a wet night, made it very difficult to keep the wheels from locking when the handbrake was applied. Once in a skid like this, it was always difficult to get them turning again without releasing the brake, which had to be done very carefully indeed to stop the engine on the right side of the junction home signal.

Although I worked on this train many times as a fireman, I always breathed a sigh of relief as we went over the river bridge and stopped at the home signal, having been fully engaged in working on the tender handbrake from Hermitage Station. Although taking into consideration the hard work put in by both firemen, especially in using the tender brake, there is no doubt that an experienced guard who knew every gradient and where to assist the driver with his handbrake was a great asset, making life a lot easier for engine crews, especially as this early morning freight train was almost always worked in darkness. The moon may be for lovers, but an engine driver looking for landmarks loves it too! Fog was always a hazard to all drivers but, on the Newbury line, it made things more difficult than ever because of the continual rise and fall of the gradients. I have worked on this line as fireman and driver when the only indication as to where we were was the sound of the wheels on the track. To all the old hands on this line, the running of the train made distinctive sounds on the rails at various points, and it was a sort of rhythm which was noticable on daylight trips and remembered to advantage in fog.

After the train had been shunted at Newbury, and its traffic detached, the train was re-formed with freight for various stations between Newbury and Winchester. The 2251 class with the same Didcot crew would then take the train forward. After leaving Newbury we would approach Enborne Junction, where we would turn off from the main line which continued from here to Westbury and Exeter. Passing Enborne Junction signal box, the fireman would take the single line token from the 'catcher', where it would have been placed by the signalman. This would be for the section to Woodhay. As can be seen from the map, stations on this route to Winchester were Woodhay, Highclere (which was actually situated in Burghclere, the name of the next station on the line), Litchfield, Whitchurch, Sutton Scotney, Kingsworthy and Winchester (Chesil). The line was similar to the Didcot to Newbury section except that the gradients were not so severe, and there were more single line 'staff' stations.

With a heavy freight train, it was a heavy pull from Enborne Junction to Highclere. The rise was, however, more gradual, and after passing Highclere it was downhill until just before reaching Burghclere. Then, after sweeping round a right-hand bend towards the home signal, it was level at the station, then up a steep rise. This short sharp 'full head of steam effort' was eventually surmounted, and the driver would shut off completely. If not required to stop at Litchfield, we would cruise at a fast speed down into Whitchurch. Looking out from the locomotive towards this station, it was surprising to see just how high the train seemed to be in relation to the station.

When running down into Whitchurch, it was again necessary to use the tender handbrake if the home signal was against you, or even if it was lowered. A tight grip had still to be kept on the wagons as just past the next signal, which might be at 'danger' due to its protection of the 'up' single line into the station, was a catch point which was controlled by the Whitchurch signalman. Several trains have come to grief at this point because they were not kept under control on the descent. From Whitchurch there was a moderate rise and then a down gradient to Sutton Scotney. If we arrived here early we would await the arrival of a passenger train, usually headed by a 2251 class engine with Western men on the footplate. We would then change over, and the Winchester men would work our freight train on while we would work their passenger train to Didcot, via Newbury and Compton.

Later on, in the early 1950s, when the Southern Region became responsible for the section south of Newbury, we would change footplates at Sutton Scotney with Eastleigh (SR) men, who would hand over their ex-LSWR Class T9 4-4-0. The first of these had been built back in 1899 by Dugald Drummond, and Southern men would not hear anything against them. To GWR men they always seemed unpredictable; perhaps we were just not used to them. Apart from the 'Aberdares', I had never before worked a passenger train with a locomotive having a steam reverser. On the Class T9s, notching up the lever sometimes did not agree with what was required.

With their very large driving wheels, these engines certainly ate up the miles although, at times, they seemed to lose more steam through the safety-valves than was being used. Also, there were occasions when however much the fireman tried, he just could not keep a good boiler of water, and it would be jumping up and down at the bottom of the boiler gauge glass. This used to give us a feeling of frustration and alarm, yet despite all this, we nearly always arrived back at Didcot on time. Upon reflection, my opinion of these engines was that they did their job, but that GWR men never really had a chance to get used to them. No. 30289 was the best of those we worked, whilst No. 30707 was the engine of which an American serviceman took a photograph whilst I was on the footplate. He was going around Europe photographing steam locomotives, and I have often wondered what he thought of minute British engines like the Class T9s, in comparison with the massive locomotives with which he was familiar.

For our part, the ex-GWR driver's instant comment might have been something along the lines of a remark I heard made by someone seeing the 3.35p.m. Didcot to Winchester train leaving, around 1959, with its three coach train. 'There's old – – – – on the corporation steamroller!' Southern men called them 'Greyhounds' and perhaps it is fitting to mention, before passing on, the exploits of the original No. 336, which covered the 112½ miles from Temple-combe to Waterloo at an average speed of 65m.p.h., back in 1904.

Sometimes on arrival at Newbury with these trains, we were scheduled to continue the journey, stopping at all stations to Reading. Here the pilot engine would take over the coaches, and we would go into Reading Shed to pick up another engine to work a passenger train to Didcot. Usually this was a BR Standard engine, its home shed being Eastleigh. On arrival at Didcot, we would take the Standard to the shed where it would be serviced for its return working, the 5.50 p.m. Didcot to Eastleigh, via Compton.

Another type of locomotive used on the Didcot to Newbury and Winchester line was the Maunsell Mogul, or the lighter mixed traffic 4-6-0s. On the GWR, there had been little to echo the other companies' post-war experiments with diesel engines although, of course, previous to that, collaboration with AEC had produced some successful diesel railcars. In the 1940s the Great Western Railway attempted to go 'one better' by ordering a gas turbine locomotive from Brown Boveri, but this venture into the future proved stillborn. Therefore the GWR retained its character well into nationalisation, with not even the new Standard classes making much impact. Among those which saw service on the Western Region were the 'Britannia' class Pacifics, the Standard 4-6-0s (Class 4 and 5), a 2-6-2T for local mixed traffic work and the large class 9F 2-10-0s. Many of the latter were actually built at Swindon including the very last one of all, named appropriately *Evening Star*.

To drivers and firemen, getting these new engines for the first time was really like being given a new toy. We knew what they were supposed to do but, somehow, in practice, it was different, as there was something about them which made us resentful and unappreciative. Many have been the times when, with my fireman, I have gone out from the shed to take over a train and my fireman, upon seeing the locomotive at its head, would mutter, 'Not a – – – – – – Standard again!' This echoed my own sentiments, but we could never analyse our feelings. From the point of view of comfort, the BR engineers had certainly made a good cab to work in, so our feelings are difficult to evaluate, unless it had something to do with the sad thought that the introduction of these locomotives was a prelude to the withdrawal of our own GWR engines. Great Western men were supremely unable to praise any other company's locomotives, and were only happy when in charge of one of their own, however ancient it may have been. Perhaps, therefore, the Standards did not have much of a chance from the start.

The mention of old engines brings me on to No. 3440 *City of Truro*, originally built in 1903, and which achieved the first recorded 100m.p.h. run the following year. It was taken out of service in 1931 and preserved in York Railway Museum until 1957, when it was restored for special work. Much to the surprise of the locomotive men at Didcot, *City of Truro* was sent to our depot to work passenger trains on the Didcot, Newbury & Southampton line when not required for special working. At the time, we had no knowledge of what took place when it was taken into Swindon Works. From a spectator's point of view, all the locomotives in a transport museum look as though they just need coal lit in the firebox for them to be off. Of course, little information as to what action is taken to preserve the locomotives, when placed in museums, is available, but it would seem obvious that boiler tubes, for instance, would be among the first items to deteriorate. Confirmation of this is at least partly suggested by the information now available from the official records, which show that *City of Truro* was actually fitted with a new standard GWR boiler at Swindon. This almost certainly accounts for the fact that this engine regularly achieved speeds well above those now allowed for larger and more modern preserved engines running on British Rail.

No one could have forseen the fantastic interest which the public took in this venture. Locomotive spotters had been much derided and belittled in some quarters, but the reappearance of this 'City' class engine proved to the general public that interest in railways was not 'kids' stuff' but an adult hobby and, of course, it has never looked back. This interest publicised the fact that *City of Truro* was working from Didcot to Southampton, and the result was quite fantastic and unexpected.

The locomotive arrived from Swindon Works at Didcot under its own steam, resplendent in the old 1903 livery, a sight which recalled to many eyes their very earliest days on the railway. The locomotive was absolutely spotless, a sight which I had not witnessed since my days at Old Oak Common when we used to clean engines in an almost competitive spirit. After a few trial trips, *City of Truro* was put into regular service. The first driver at Didcot to take charge of the machine was asked by reporters for his judgement of the engine's performance, and he remarked that 'it went like a bird'! Certainly, the locomotive gave all that was asked of it.

On the second week I and my fireman, Gordon Burridge, were working the 7.38 Didcot to Southampton service and, accordingly, were booked engine No. 3440 for the job (in Swindon Museum, *City of Truro* has reverted to the number 3717 and the 1906 livery, which is more strictly correct in view of its technical condition). When booking on duty, and drawing the usual equipment from the stores, I felt that this was just another engine that required oiling, and the only difference from an ordinary day's work was that it was a lot cleaner than usual but, I was wrong! The journey to Newbury was devoid of anything unusual, except for some admiring comments from our passengers, but at Newbury an avalanche of photographers descended upon us from all vantage points adjacent to the station and also on the platform. Cameras of all description, some on tripods (the point of which I have never quite understood) were in action; this was a real novelty, so Gordon and I endeavoured to get 'in the picture' where we could. Some of the photographers wanted a live picture, which included the driver and fireman, and I would ask these to send me a copy, although some did not need to be asked.

After a short break at Newbury we were off again, stopping at all stations to Winchester. By now, it seemed that the word had gone along the grassy banks, in the cuttings and at every station, batteries of cameras were waiting for us. Undoubtedly *City of Truro* was proving a great attraction, which was quite fantastic when one considers that other GWR locomotives such as *King George V* had not, then at least, received such recognition. Now, of course, we recognise exactly the same events every time one of the preserved steam locomotives runs on the main line.

At Winchester, I was interested to see three art students from the local college who were sat comfortably on the platform with their drawing boards, on which they commenced to draw immediately we came out of the tunnel and into Winchester Station. One of them told me that they proposed to spend all of one week at the station, at the appropriate time, to draw our locomotive!

After Winchester comes Shawford Junction, where we left the Western Region line and ran on to the Southern Region where we continued stopping at all stations to Southampton Terminus. Enthusiasm on the Southern lines was not so marked, which is perhaps understandable considering the rivalry that had existed between the four main line companies, and which lived on beyond 1948. Even so, at Eastleigh, the scene was just like before with cameras everywhere, except that now we began to be asked questions about the engines capabilities and its history. I could only reply that the engine performed perfectly, which it did. Gordon was a first class fireman so we were quite clean and not covered in coal dust, as is sometimes the case with an inefficient fireman. The thought comes to mind that perhaps the Eastleigh workmen's sight of a real engine was so rare that they thought this was the latest thing from Swindon! Our 'welcome' at Southampton Terminus was really something to remember; there were cameras everywhere. Also, when we arrived at Southampton Depot to turn the engine for the homeward journey, the cameras were again out in force.

For the five days that we worked this train we were given No. 3440, and every day the engine performed very satisfactorily. At the end of the week we were still being photographed, and I have no doubt that during the following week the new engine crew had similar experiences.

I have in this narrative mentioned, from time to time, the firemen who worked with me in my driving days. Looking back on those years I think that I had some very good firemen, which allowed me to concentrate on my job of handling the locomotive and running to time. Writing about *City of Truro* gives me an opportunity to pay a small tribute to my fireman of that time, Gordon Burridge. I soon found that he was a very efficient fireman, a member of the Didcot Mutual Improvement Class who had learned a great deal about the locomotive. Also, it seemed that during his time as a fireman he had been very observant of signals; indeed, his knowledge of different routes was almost as good as my own, and this was of considerable assistance in our work together. Signal positions were sometimes difficult to see through steam and smoke, but a knowledgeable fireman elminated many of these difficulties although, of course, it was the driver who was actually responsible for seeing them. To be able to rely on one's fireman without any doubts was, however, a great asset. I have had the doubtful experience, on more than one occasion, of being told a particular signal was at 'line clear', only to find that this was not the case. However, with Gordon Burridge, I never had this problem because he was never wrong. Gordon later died in very sad circumstances, on returning from a holiday in Spain.

As an engine driver, I was very familiar with the Didcot to Newbury and Southampton line and, indeed, like the older men, I could say that I knew almost every sleeper from Didcot to Winchester. Today, the Newbury line does not exist. The southern section was closed in 1960, bringing to an end the sojourn of *City of Truro* at Didcot, the remainder in 1962 after the service had been reduced to a one car diesel multiple unit. Where once the gleaming metals stretched away up the incline from Didcot to Upton and Churn — a station surrounded on all sides by the Berkshire Downs — and beyond, where the sun reflected back the rails like burnished silver, everything is gone; all that is left are memories. Memories, perhaps, not of Class T9s or of *City of Truro* but of 2251 class 0-6-0s, struggling manfully along and belching smoke and red hot cinders from their chimneys, causing unceasing concern to the farmers through whose land the railway wound its snakelike way. Although the line is no longer there, in the quiet of the evening you will plainly hear trains disappearing in the distance. They are not actually on the Newbury line of course but, from my back garden, they sound very much as though the are battling with the gradient up to Churn.

CHAPTER SEVEN

Having made numerous journeys as an engine driver and a fireman, I have had many strange experiences, and several have stayed in my memory. One in particular which I recall occurred at Hungerford. After making up a train on the 'down' side, we were required to convey a wagon containing a car to the 'up' side unloading dock. In order to get there, points had to be used employing levers which could not be operated until a key, obtained from the signalman, had been inserted into the hole of a box-like receptacle about 2ft. square, the keyhole being circular and about 3in. in diameter. This brings me to the curious part of my story. You must understand that this box was not used more than once a day and, on some days, was never opened at all. Therefore, except for the keyhole, it was completely shut and yet, in one corner of it, I found a beautifully made bird's nest containing ten perfectly formed eggs. How did the bird build its nest, and how did it carry the grass which formed the nest into that place? I really do not know.

The most extraordinary experience that I can remember could have happened to anyone, as I was a passenger at the time. I had taken a train up to Wolverhampton and was returning as a passenger. As the train ran into the platform and came to a stand I saw that it was very crowded, and there were at least 150 people waiting with me to board it. However, I had had a long day, and was determined to get a seat. I grasped a door handle but, just at that moment, a very large woman stepped on my foot, barged past me and got into the train. The station staff were literally packing the people in like sardines to get the train away on time, so I limped aboard.

After limping up and down the corridors with the others, I finally found a compartment occupied by a man and, on the other side, majestically occupying the whole seat, a very large alsatian dog. The dog's owner was calmly reading the *Sporting Life*, completely oblivious to anything outside his own little world. I had had a very long day, and my foot was still protesting about the rough treatment that it had received, so I opened the door to the compartment and sat down without bothering to enquire as to whether all the seats in the compartment had been reserved. After a few miles, the dog's owner jumped up suddenly, saying 'I'll just pop along for a drink; look after the dog for me will you?' With that he was gone.

I am not really a 'doggy' person, having not, until very recently, had very much to do with that species of animal, so you can imagine that I was at a bit of a loss. The alsatian now gave me a menacing snarl, and rose on to his hind legs as though stretching. I decided that I needed a cigarette, but, as my hand moved towards my pocket, the dog rose to his full height and growled. He then stepped down off the seat and stood looking at me with a baleful eye, or so it seemed to me. I cannot really say that I was frightened but I was certainly perturbed. All at once, with his examination over, he climbed back on to the cushions and lay down. I did not move and, at last, the dog's owner returned and said, 'Well, old boy, I'm glad to see that you kept quiet!' I am not really sure whether he was referring to me or the dog, but I felt like rushing along the corridor and having a long cold drink for myself! Perhaps the windy, rocking cab of a locomotive is to be preferred after all to the comforts of being a passenger!

One line where this was certainly not so was the one between Oxford and Worcester. My experience of this line usually began at about 6.55a.m. with a commuter train for Paddington, as the roster had us working back a Worcester express over the full length of the line from the terminus. The engine on the 'up' train would usually be a 'Hall', prepared for us by shed men. We would take it off shed, couple it to the coaches and then, at 7.10 a.m., we would get the 'right away', and start our 400 ton 'all stations' train to Reading and then to Paddington.

A great many of the passngers on these early morning trains would have their 'own' position to stand on the platform, and also what they regarded as their 'own' compartment in the train — and woe betide anyone who sat in 'their' seat — so if the driver stopped the train about a yard from where they were standing, they would not get on, but would walk back to where 'their compartment' was! Indeed, I have seen this happen even when the train had, through some inadvertance, arrived a few minutes late. Also, these were the very people who, should the train arrive a few minutes late at Paddington through permanent way checks or signals, give the driver a really foul look as they passed the engine. The reader must not get the impression that enginemen have a grudge against passengers, but I was always impressed on entering Paddington to see, in the seats along the various platforms, people whose facial expressions seem to indicate that the railway timetable should be altered to suit the time of their arrival at the station.

The big thing at Paddington to 'new boy' drivers was the ability to stop a train with his engine about a yard or so from the stop blocks at the end of the platform. So quickly does the train fill up the space that the first few times that I did this I felt that I would stop short or overrun, but I soon learned how it was done, and it became very much a second nature.

After being relieved at Paddington, my fireman would make a can of tea and then we would go along to the Worcester train which, in those days, left at 9.15a.m. It was usually headed by a 'Castle' or occasionally a 'Hall', and on some occasions my fireman — usually Tom Edwards on these jobs — would find that he had relieved an inexperienced fireman, and would have great difficulty in maintaining the steam level. Although quite tightly scheduled, once he had begun to achieve success from his own experience, the first part of the journey was reasonably comfortable. Even so, there could be no let up on my part, as a couple of minutes lost would be extremely difficult to regain.

After going round the north curve at Didcot the story began to change, for the going became tougher. Through Oxford, Handborough, Charlbury (where we would take water from the troughs), Ascott-under-Wychwood and Shipton, we would be on a rising gradient; through Kingham and on to Moreton-in-Marsh, where there was a permanent 50m.p.h. check, we would be on a falling gradient to Blockley, and the fireman would be able to wipe some of the sweat and coal dust from his face and have a short breather. For passenger trains, the next stage of the journey was relatively easy, involving a heavy pull up to Chipping Campden and then down through Honeybourne Tunnel. We would approach the tunnel at 60m.p.h. and, at the exit, after having held the engine back, we would be doing 80 m.p.h. This would be continued down through Honeybourne Station.

For freight trains, the position was somewhat different. At Chipping Campden we would be stopped to allow sufficient handbrakes to be put on by the guard, so that the driver would pull the train down through the tunnel rather than risk the wagons picking up and pushing the train to an uncontrollable speed. Even with this precaution, sometimes due to moisture on the rails in the tunnel and, in the autumn, falling leaves blown from the trees on the surrounding embankments, the engine would skid alarmingly. With the weight of the train pushing from behind, we would gather speed until the application of engine and van brakes, together with the use of the sanding gear, brought the train under control. The noise of a freight train running normally in a tunnel is quite different to that of a train skidding; there is none of the rhythm of sound made by the moving parts of the locomotive, and all is an eerie silence of foreboding.

Passenger trains would not experience this problem although on the return journey the position might be a little different. After Evesham, the fireman would be getting his fire ready to take us up through the tunnel. Although working on a passenger train the possibility of failing in the tunnel never really occurred to us, although we knew that even a 'Castle' or a 'Hall' would have to be worked very hard indeed to maintain speed to the exit at Chipping Campden. After that, for a short distance, there was the downhill stretch, and a heavy pull to Moreton-in-Marsh and thereafter the going would be the reverse of the 'down' journey. On arrival at Oxford we would be relieved by other men, as this train did not stop at Didcot.

Memories of journeys such as this leads, naturally, on to the question of what is the best recollection of one's working life. Others will have different ideas, but for me I would say that the time spent travelling the GWR 'learning the road' would be my choice. This included making oneself familiar with all signals, permanent way checks, speed restrictions and signal boxes along a route, in preparation for driving trains along it.

To do this, it was first necessary to be accepted on to the footplate. This was entirely the prerogative of the driver, although on express trains it was not always convenient to have a third man on a steam engine footplate. There were a number of things which could make a driver refuse to co-operate, such as bad coal causing his fireman extra work; but they very rarely refused. When standing behind the driver, it was possible to get practically the same view of the signals as he and if he was so inclined, he would help by pointing out, wherever possible, 'your' signals on a particular gantry. Since some of these gantries carried fifteen signals, that was useful information. Of course, this was not always possible, as many signals were passed at speeds of 70m.p.h. and, with the driver concentrating on his job, he simply had to leave the visitor to find out for himself.

It was not the actual learning of the road which was so relishing an experience, but that of travelling at high speeds on the Great Western Railway's finest locomotives. When driving, it was just a race against the clock, but as a driver learning the road one was able to calmly realise and appreciate the experience of the ultimate achievement, and of sharing the footplate of a massive express passenger locomotive doing 80m.p.h. When driving the same engines to the same timetables, there would not be the time to indulge in this appreciation in quite the same way.

Of course, we were always told that the passenger link was the ultimate in a driver's responsibilities, but I cannot agree with this.

To be working trains in direct contact with the travelling public was, of course, a responsibility, but from a point of view of train handling, it was always my opinion that the loose-coupled freight trains and the part vacuum-fitted trains were the hardest to handle. The very high speeds attained by passenger trains, and the stopping at stations in an exact position to enable passengers to board the train required skill and judgement, but a continuous brake on the locomotive and every coach was of great assistance, and was not available to freight train drivers.

A passenger train driver carried an enormous amount of prestige and, therefore, it was 75 per cent of a driver's desire to attain the 'top hat link'. However, this did not mean that it was necessarily the hardest work. There was no small responsibility, for instance, in working 'running in duties'. In the days when the main line eastwards from Swindon to Didcot included a halt at Stratton Park, as well as stations at Shrivenham, Uffington, Challow, Wantage Road and Steventon, this was an ideal line for such turns. All types of locomotive, including the 'King' and 'Castle' classes and, later on, the Swindon-built batch of 'Britannias' were tried out on this 24 mile stretch of line. The driver would carry with him very substantial quantities of oil and at each station he would be turned off the main line, giving him ample opportunity to examine bearings, axleboxes and other parts of the engine which were, in any way, likely to show signs of runnning hot or some other problem. If an axlebox did run hot he could refill it with oil and carry on at reduced speed and, being a 'light engine', he could return to base without upsetting the timetable. On some of these 'light engine' workings very high speeds were sometimes achieved. The story goes that on one such run, a 'Saint' on which Collett, the Chief Mechanical Engineer, was actually riding, was worked up to about 120m.p.h.! This was, however, in the opposite direction, west of Swindon.

After a couple of light engine trips, engines would be put on to local passenger trains running from Swindon to Didcot. No great speed would be maintained for very long, and examination at stations would reveal any apparent problems. Due to this, the 6.05 stopping train from Didcot to Swindon often boasted super power, far in excess of the demands of the load or the timetable.

The different performance characteristics of the various types of GWR locomotive were very noticeable; the pannier tanks did not like sharp bends in the track while the 6300 class Moguls, when under stress, would literally roll from side to side. The 1944-built 'County' class 4-6-0s always felt like they were running on a rockbed, and lying heavily on the rails. This was, in the early days, a serious problem, which caused Swindon some considerable heartache and may even, according to one writer, have had some part in setting off the rather unofficial Pacific proposal of the 1940s.

Inevitably, the tender engine type with which we mostly came into contact with was the 'Hall' class. One of our Didcot jobs, on which we would be rostered one of these engines, was to Oxley Yard, just beyond Wolverhampton. We would relieve men from Westbury at Didcot North, on an Exeter to Crewe vacuum goods train. The engine, having worked through from Exeter, was usually very short of coal and the fire, in consequence, was very dirty, and required considerable skill on the part of the fireman to maintain pressure. In a situation such as this we would arrange with Birmingham Control, before leaving Didcot, to take on coal at Banbury, and also to have the fire cleaned. This meant that we had to struggle on a gruelling uphill haul from Didcot to Banbury, but I always considered that if the Westbury men could get to Didcot, via Newbury and Compton, we could manage to Banbury.

On the good days, when there was plenty of coal in the tender and the engine was steaming perfectly, we could roar through Banbury in 35 minutes from Didcot, and face the rising gradient to Fenny Compton. From there it was downhill to Leamington, and passing through here I would glance at the station clock and note that we were keeping good time. Then came the really heavy part of the road.

Through Warwick, I would gradually increase the regulator opening until, as we passed Hatton Station, it would be wide open with the cut off at 35 per cent. The pressure valves at each cylinder head would be spitting steam; a certain sign that the engine was under severe pressure. The road would then ease to Lapworth, but 45m.p.h. had to be maintained to enable us to pick up water over the troughs at Rowington. Solihull was soon passed, and my fireman would be able to relax a little as we entered the maze of track intersections which heralded our approach to the outskirts of Birmingham.

At Bordesley, we would detach wagons containing livestock or produce for Birmingham, then after re-forming our train, we would pull up to Bordesley North where we would await signals to proceed back on to the main line once again. On our far right, express passenger trains would be continuously passing on the main line whilst the local trains used the relief lines to run into Moor Street, then a subsidiary station to Snow Hill.

With a suitable margin between trains, the signalman would give us 'line clear'. Wasting no time, I would immediately start out on to the main line and head through Snow Hill Tunnel. On occasions we would be brought to a stand on the through line, in the middle of this station, whilst a passenger train left from an adjoining platform or bay for Wolverhampton. Once we got under way again we would soon be passing Soho, with Winson Green Prison away to our right.

It is a pity that so few young people use the railways today, for they provide a real education in history, geography, economics and many other subjects which are usually the bane of their lives. For instance, the scene after leaving Didcot, on each side of the line, is a panorama of green fields, cultivated land and grazing animals, which hardly give way to Oxford, Banbury or Leamington, but approaching Birmingham, from about Tyseley, rows of tenements back on to each side of the line, and then industrial works, car and component factories provide the scenery, with a considerable area of land being taken up by railway installations. The green grass and wild flowers give way to a man-made vista and a dirty smokey atmosphere which is the result of the age of heavy industry and mass production. It would stay like this for miles and miles, past Birmingham and beyond Wolverhampton, including the Hawthorns, Priestfield and Swan Village, three stations whose names utterly belied their surroundings. Of Swan Village, George Behrend, in his fine book *Gone With Regret*, said, '... any self-respecting swan has long ago flown elsewhere from that canal hard by the gasholders, whose water looks as though its chemical analysis would turn out to be something quite different to H_2O'. There are many lessons for today's youth in the West Midlands.

This job to Oxley with a 'Hall' was a very arduous day's work for driver and fireman and, I always felt, an achievement on its completion. There were, however, jobs on this line that necessitated 'double home' working. I should explain that a 'double home' turn of duty was when, after working a train to its destination, the engine crew took their locomotive to shed and booked off duty and, after a period of rest, either at a railwayman's hostel or at a private lodging, they would book on again, usually the next day, and work a train back to their home depot. While some men liked this sort of work, the majority were very much against it. There were a variety of reasons for this, the principle one being that men did not want to be away from their families. There were also complaints about the conditions in some of the places where the men were supposed to lodge. Our union demanded better facilities, and so the GWR began to build hostels, or to take over property for this purpose.

My first experience of 'double home' work was with the 1.05a.m. Swindon to Bordesley freight, a turn of duty in which we were required to book off at Tyseley after having taken the engine to the shed. The 'double home' lodge here was classed as a hostel but, in actual fact, it was a converted dogs' home, or so it was said! It was quite an experience to sleep away from home as the driver, fireman and guard all slept in the same room. Whilst there was a lot to be desired about this hostel, the Company always contended that plans for a completely new building were in hand. In due course of time this was, in fact, built and it was a revelation of what could be done for the men. Each man had his own individual room with a built-in wardrobe, table, chair and so on. The bed had a luxuriously deep and well-sprung mattress and there were washrooms, baths, showers and even electric sockets in the walls for shavers. Personally, I could not fault anything. In fact, the men were so proud of this building that certain rooms were designated as 'lounges', and no one was allowed to enter in their overalls.

The train back, usually headed by a 'Hall', an LMS class 8F 2-8-0 or even an 'Austerity' freight engine, was often loaded up to the full capacity of the locomotive. At Tyseley, we would come off the main line on to the Henley-in-Arden line through Stratford-upon-Avon, and so to Honeybourne and that tunnel again. Many are the times that the air in that tunnel has been black with smoke and fumes and, with a poor steaming engine, we were always wondering, as steam pressure fell, if we were going to have to stop, or rather, if we were going to come to a stand. Somehow, however, we always came through. What a story a fireman could write of such a trip; they might have thought that some of their drivers were maniacs, but when they became a driver themselves, they would soon learn the necessity of what was done.

CHAPTER EIGHT

Although now retired for over ten years, my connection with the railway has not ended. Apart from weekly contacts with the retired section of the Didcot Staff Association, my wife and I are still fairly regular travellers on British Rail (Western Region). However, today, Western locomotive power has changed out of all recognition to what it was even ten years ago, when the diesel-hydraulics were supreme. Now, in the early 1980s, we are carried to our children and grandchildren by the luxurious Inter-City 125 trains, a new world in train travel as far as my experience goes.

Sitting in the air-conditioned and vibration free Inter-City 125 units, enjoying the stable ride which is only slightly spoilt by the swaying on points and crossings, and while passing towns, stations and depots of which I can say that I know every inch, my mind sometimes goes back to my years at the front end. Comparisons are inevitable, although there is really none between the cushioned comfort of the passenger side of the HSTs and the driving cab of a steam engine. I have no experience of these trains nor, for that matter, of motor cars, lorries or boats, and I have no idea what the operators of these vehicles may feel when driving them. Yet, when preparing a steam engine for a trip, whether the day was hot, wet or cold, I always felt that oiling a locomotive was like feeding a horse or a dog on a leash, like an animal always straining to be away and do one's bidding.

In later years, when we were booked to take an engine from Paddington or from Old Oak Common Yard to the shed, a lump would seem to come into my throat as I would look around at the all too familiar scenes, especially when I was greeted by many of my old workmates and by the Running Foreman as 'Alf'. Invariably, of course, we had been cleaners together, and I would know them better than anyone actually working in the place! To many of my firemen, taking them to Old Oak Common locomotive depot was like giving them a day's outing and those who had been born at Didcot were astonished at the size of the depot, in comparison to Didcot's own shed. We would prepare an engine — a 'Hall' or a 'Castle' — and go off shed, tender first, via the overbridge at Old Oak Common, to Paddington's departure side. The guard would give us the weight and number of coaches, and we would then have about fifteen minutes for a cup of tea and some sandwiches.

There was not a lot the fireman could do to the fire in the firebox in Paddington Station, due to the rule about making smoke because of the glass roof, but there was plenty that he could do to make his trip easier. This included getting more coal forward, breaking it up into a nice size and, if he thought it was going to be necessary, and it usually was, to get the long poker down off the tender rack ready for use.

Ironically, with a 'Castle' class engine and seven coaches, such as we would have on the Worcester jobs, there would not be any problems in maintaining steam pressure or in running to time. It might be a different matter on the heavier jobs to Bristol or the West of England, but express passenger work at Didcot rarely included those routes.

Leaving Paddington dead on time, obeying the permanent speed restrictions for running out of the platforms and passing Royal Oak Station, I would gradually increase speed. At Westbourne Park a glance across to my fireman would indicate that everything was all right, that he was just working normally and building up the fire. When passing Old Oak Common, I would begin to lift the regulator to increase speed and, without any effort, the engine would respond and passing Acton, we would be up to 55m.p.h. On our right was Acton Yard, where I did some of my very early work as a fireman. Through Ealing Broadway our speed would increase to Southall, where a glance at the roof-top clock on the AEC factory ('Makers of London's Buses') would indicate that we were running to time.

With the reversing lever cut-off back to 20 per cent, the steam simmering at the safety-valves, the footplate swept clean and the coal in the tender watered, it would look like being a good trip. The fireman could wipe his hands, sit down on his seat and finish his sandwiches. We never said very much to each other because, on fast trains, it sometimes happened that the fireman would see a signal before his driver, so we would refrain from distracting each other. All the way from Southall, with the new locomotive shed on the left and with the huge EMI building on the 'up' side at Hayes, it would be factories on either side.

The fireman's rest period did not last very long as on the approach to Slough he would begin to make up the fire again. We would roar through Slough Station at about 70m.p.h. and, immediately afterwards, I would shut the regulator for a speed restriction at Burnham. Immediately, a black pall of smoke from the chimney would blanket the Horlicks building as we passed. At Maidenhead we passed over Brunel's famous flat arch Thames Bridge, although neither engine crew or passengers are able to appreciate the sight of those supposedly incredible structures.

Reading was the first stop and then we would move on to Didcot East Junction, where I would have to check down to 40m.p.h. for the crossover from the 'down' main line to the Oxford line. On our left, as we approached Didcot North Junction, was Didcot Shed. After Didcot North, I could open up and increase speed, rapidly passing Appleford Crossing and then the wooden platforms at Appleford Halt. Then through Culham, with the disused hangars of the Royal Naval Air Station on the right. We would now be passing Radley at 70m.p.h. where, on other days, we might stop to allow passengers to 'Change Here For Abingdon'. At Kennington Junction, we would be reducing speed again for the 50m.p.h. permanent speed restriction over the river bridge and into Oxford Station. The majority of passengers on these Worcester trains alighted here as even thirty years ago, trains beyond, on the line to Worcester, ran comparatively empty.

After leaving Oxford it was difficult to increase speed very much, as at Wolvercote Junction there was a sharp curve with a permanent speed restriction of 40m.p.h. From this point on to Kingham the line was at a rising gradient, and although it was not severe, it was one which severely tested a freight engine with a heavy load, as I have already mentioned, but in this instance our 'Castle' could ignore it completely. At Bruen Crossing, we might get a cheery wave from the signalman as the whistle was sounded.

On these journeys, there could be one of those incidents which made every steam job different. I remember that, on one occasion, my fireman had lowered the water scoop and had filled the tank whilst over the troughs at Goring, but we decided to have another fill as we passed over the set of water-troughs at Charlbury, just after the station where we had previously stopped. Although quite efficient and well-versed in this manoeuvre, he was unable to wind up the scoop, due to the onrush of the water, so I left the controls and turned round to help him. We did manage to get the scoop out and locked in the shut position, but we were unable to stop the overflow of water coming out from the back of the tender. This meant that a mushroom of water swept down and over the coal on to the footplate, at the same time bringing down lumps of coal. I managed to clamber on to my seat, out of the way, and carried on driving, but my fireman had to spend the next ten minutes clearing up the water and coal from the footplate. A moment previous it had been clean and tidy but between us we had managed to save the water scoop from damage.

After Kingham came Adlestrop, better known today perhaps to the readers of Edward Thomas than to railway enthusiasts. This is

Cotswold country, the real countryside, with farmland and animals on either side of the line. Then came Moreton-in-Marsh and Blockley Crossing where we would pick up speed, passing through Chipping Campden Station at 60m.p.h., and into that tunnel again. We would shoot out of the tunnel at the other end at about 80m.p.h., with steam shut off, through Honeybourne Station and down through the Vale of Evesham to Norton Junction, and finally into Worcester (Shrub Hill) Station. This was a peculiar station that always seemed to me, with signals at each end, some with catch points, and goods yard and locomotive shed all crowded together, as though the builders had run out of room in which to do a reasonable job. On those turns we would work a midday train, hauled by a 'Hall', back as far as Oxford. Around Evesham, in the summer, there was row upon row of runner beans in the 'up' side fields while at Pershore, plums hung over the 'down' platform. Many an engine crew has judged the position on the platform of their train by the nearness of the rear of the tender to those overhanging fruits!

When approaching the long climb towards Honeybourne Tunnel I would increase the regulator opening to gain more effort, because this gradient continued right through the tunnel to just past Chipping Campden Station. Going down it was to your advantage, but when coming back it was a different story. When passing through the tunnel, the engine would begin to bark, with the cut-off as far back as possible, but it was really an exaggeration of sound. On freight trains and with locomotives which, to say the least, had seen better days, we realised the real meanness of Honeybourne Tunnel. If, with a passenger train, there was ever any doubt about the steaming quality of the locomotive, the policy was always to use the Honeybourne stop to regain a full head of steam. There was, of course, a banking engine kept at Honeybourne, but with a good engine on a passenger train it was rarely used.

After Moreton-in-Marsh and Kingham, and round Wolvercote Junction to Oxford, we would leave the train here and return to Didcot 'on the cushions'. It was a hard day's work but, as my fireman once said, 'the results were excellent, plenty of steam and the right time everywhere. A good day's work indeed.'

Millions of words have been written about the steam engine and, no doubt, many more will be written. As far as I am concerned, the post-war years were marked by three major events; nationalisation, the end of steam, and the maturing of the modernisation plan. Although most of us had voted for nationalisation in 1945, we were bitter about the abolition of the GWR Rule Book. Of course, a standardised national rule book had to be introduced but some men at different locomotive sheds were so incensed by some of the new rules that strike action was suggested. It was felt that some of these rules were not up to the safety standards of the GWR Rule Book. To quote one example, under the GWR, where permanent way track improvements which necessitated trains travelling at reduced speed were in operation, the distant signal would be kept at 'caution' for trains entering the section, as a reminder to the driver of the track work ahead for which he would need to reduce speed. It can be readily seen that on a journey of perhaps 150 miles, it was quite possible that a driver would have seven or eight of these restrictions to deal with. Although being in possession of his speed restriction book the driver could not refer to it when travelling at speed, so the distant signal at 'caution' was a reminder of the need to reduce speed. This was very useful, bearing in mind that an express train could be approaching a speed check at 80m.p.h., particularly when many locomotives were not fitted with speedometers. Under the BR ruling, this precaution was abolished, and all distant signals for entering a restricted section were kept at 'line clear'. The GWR locomotive men protested that it was too much to ask of an express train driver, on long distance journeys, to remember a multitude of speed checks, particularly at night. However, British Railways would not withdraw the ruling so it became, along with other rules, operative on the Western Region.

The locomotive men's daily work sheets were altered to an entirely new format, and repair cards were introduced for booking repairs on locomotives. This was, of course, a driver's duty when bringing an engine to shed, with the cards being handed to the foreman when booking off. This again was contrary to GWR practice as the GWR system was that all repairs were entered in a repair book in duplicate. The driver's report page was handed to the mechanical foreman who would instruct his staff to carry out the necessary work, while the carbon copy of the repairs booked by the driver remained in the book, which always remained accessible to all drivers. The advantage with the GWR system was that when booking on duty to prepare an engine for a trip, a driver could always examine the repair book to see if any work had been entered by the previous driver. The British Railways' card repair system made this impossible and left one man, the Running Foreman, with the final word as to what repairs were to be done to an engine. With the shortage of steam locomotives experienced on occasions by the Western Region, one wonders how often an engine was put back into service with just the bare necessities of repairs carried out.

However, these new systems came and stayed — at least for the rest of my service. One innovation introduced in 1948 which has, apparently, not stood the test of time is the placing of the shed number code on a metal plate at the bottom of the smokebox door. The GWR had an easily recognisable letter code; for example, SLO was Slough and DID was Didcot. It is ironic that, in recent years, the 'new' code has been abolished and replaced by a letter code which hardly differs at all, as far as the Western Region is concerned, from that in force before 1948!

The dieselisation of the Western Region started in 1958, and carried on at ever increasing speed from about 1960. Many steam drivers tried to opt out of this programme, but everyone had to learn the new ways. For the younger drivers this was not too difficult, but men in their sixties found that it was like starting all over again. Yet here was a machine that, when put on heavy main line freight trains, always had power at the ready without the need to shovel in coal to maintain a fire. Another aspect of the diesels, which drivers instantly appreciated, was the clear view of the signals from the cab. On a steam locomotive, if a signal was placed awkwardly, the driver might well have to go across the cab — getting in the fireman's way — to see it properly. This would mean leaving the controls and again, as sometimes happened on the engines with larger boilers, he would have to lean out from the side of the cab to see a signal at all. Another advantage, and one which I think carried a lot of weight with enginemen, was that on a diesel there was no clambering about in the motion to oil valve gear, and there were no dirty overalls for one's wife to wash as we now worked in a smart blue uniform!

Despite this, ex-Great Western men were upset by some of the results of this change-over. It was one thing to know in your mind, that, in the future, one's job was going to be done much more efficiently, but to see locomotives like the 'King' and 'Castle' classes destroyed to bring this about was more than many men could let pass without caustic comment. There is absolutely no doubt at all that many of the locomotives sent to the scrap yard could have worked on for a good number of years, and there is some evidence that BR's engineering team believed so too. It was one thing for early engines such as *Caerphilly Castle* (built 1923, withdrawn 1960) or *Pendennis Castle* (built 1924, withdrawn 1964) to be taken out of service, but the later engines built in the 1940s — the 'Castle' class from No. 5098 onwards and the 'Modified Halls' had a very short railway life of, at the most, twenty and, in some cases, less than fifteen years. If we bear in mind that the Great Western Railway, in particular, broke up locomotives after a relatively short life, these years of service are still short. On average, the 'Star' and 'Saint' class locomotives remained in service for about 38 years, far longer than the later passenger engines built at Swindon. What actual justification for the wholesale squandering of these resources can there possibly be? As it was, the years up to 1965 were very sad and frustrating ones.

Looking back from even a few years later, from the comfort of a diesel driver in his heated cab who could, with the merest action of the flicking of a switch, clear the observation windows of snow, ice and rain, and remembering how, in the winter, my fireman and I would try to clear the spectacle windows of snow and ice and peer through them to locate signals, whilst all around was a white blanket, shrouded, perhaps, by darkness, certainly by the smoke from our engine, I knew that I never wanted to go back to those steam days.

One of the last steam jobs which I worked was in the late summer of 1965, when I had No. 6937 *Conynghan Hall* on the last leg of the Salop parcels train from Didcot to Paddington. By then this engine, along with all its fellows, had lost its nameplates as a precaution against thieves. I have never been able to quite understand who it was who was stealing these nameplates, as although there were instances of a few so-called enthusiasts making off with railway property, I would have thought that most of them would have realised that what they had stolen they could never actually show, since most people would have realised how it had been obtained. No, I think that scrap metal merchants interested in the copper and brass were possibly responsible for some of these incidents. Anyway, *Conyngham Hall* was without nameplates, and had little in the way of maintenance done to it. No one could have cleaned it for a very long time, and it looked a very sad sight indeed. It was a sad way for the great locomotives of a once great railway to go out. Perhaps, however, that is the way of the world; it is the children and the new things which get the distinction, and maybe that is how it should be. However, it cannot be long and indeed, the time may even be upon us, when an entirely new generation of railwaymen will have arisen whose careers on the railway started after the extinction of the steam locomotive. Theirs may be a better railway, but they will have missed something which was of great importance to GWR engine crews, and which seems to be sadly lacking today — pride in the job.

Above: The author on the footplate of 'Hall' class No. 6937, on the 'up' Shrewsbury parcels train in July 1965. This was one of the last steam workings handled by Didcot locomen.   *L. A. Summers*

Below: The final rites! In January 1966, the author has a last look at the engines which he drove for 25 years, and which are now all withdrawn from service.   *L. A. Summers*